An Okinawan KITCHEN

HAWAI'I Cooks

Traditional Recipes with an Island Twist

GRANT SATO

Photography by
Kaz Tanabe

Mutual Publishing

To Grandma

This book is a reflection of a lifetime of your unconditional love and the lasting memories of the great times we spent together, eating, drinking, and traveling. You are the joy in my life and I look forward to many more memorable moments with you.

Library of Congress Control Number: 2014938662

ISBN: 978-1939487-37-7

All photography by Kaz Tanabe, unless otherwise noted
Art direction by Grant Sato
Okinawan props provided by Grant Sato
Cover design by Jane Gillespie
Interior design by Courtney Tomasu

First Printing, August 2014
Second Printing, August 2016
Third Printing, September 2018

Mutual Publishing, LLC
1215 Center Street, Suite 210
Honolulu, Hawai'i 96816
Ph: 808-732-1709 / Fax: 808-734-4094
email: info@mutualpublishing.com
www.mutualpublishing.com
Printed in South Korea

Photo on page x © Dennis Oda, *Honolulu Star-Advertiser*

Photos from Dreamstime.com: pg. iii © Buriy, pg. iv © Yulia Davidovich, pg. viii © Timhesterphotography, pg. xii © Eyeblink, pg. xiii © Baibaz, pg. 4 © Aas2009, pg. 6 © Panyukova Uliana, pg. 8 © Vlntn, pg. 12 © Elena Elisseeva, pg. 13 © Photodee, pg. 17 © Danil Roudenko, pg. 21 © Carmen Steiner, pg. 29 © Baloncici, pg. 30 (eggs) © Branislav Senic, pg. 30 (tofu), 117 © Ukrphoto, pg. 30 (bitter melon) © Torsakarin, pg. 51 © Hanhanpeggy, pg. 55 (photo frame) © Probordersandframes, pg. 59 © Marek Uliasz, pg. 74 © Martinjaud, pg. 86 © Alian226, pg. 87 © Alfio Scisetti, pg. 97 © Efired, pg. 105 © Linqong, pg. 108 © Govindji, pg. 113 (photo frame) © Tankas, pg. 116 © Moori, pg. 135 © Vladimir Blinov

Honolulu Star ★ Advertiser

An *Okinawan Kitchen* is the third in a series of cookbooks partnering Mutual Publishing and the *Honolulu Star-Advertiser* in an exploration of Hawai'i's many ethnic cuisines.

For Grant Sato, chef-instructor at Kapi'olani Community College, cooking is a career. For Grant Sato, grandson of Jeanette Setsuko Akamine, cooking is a passion that binds him to his family, his home in Hawai'i, and his Okinawan heritage.

An Okinawan Kitchen celebrates all these connections. In this cookbook Grant pays tribute to the skills taught him by his grandmother and expands on them with dishes based on his culinary training and his travels to Okinawa and Japan.

At its heart this book is a guide to a colorful, yet often overlooked, cuisine, as it has evolved in our islands. It is Grant's hope—and ours—that these dishes will become favorites on your family's table.

At the *Honolulu Star-Advertiser* we celebrate the diversity of island cuisine every week on our Food pages. We are proud to build on that tradition with the series *Hawai'i Cooks*.

Dennis Francis
President and publisher,
Honolulu Star-Advertiser and O'ahu Publications

Contents

Okinawan Basics

Goya

Pork

Fish

Contemporary Creations

Acknowledgments

Funny how all of my memories are tied to smells and tastes. Just catching a hint of a familiar aroma or taste takes me back to the moment I experienced it for the first time—from the smell of senko in Ojiji's Kahaluʻu house to the joy of eating sweet, savory, and juicy, rafute with charred musubi in Okinawa. Writing this book has helped me reconnect with those great times and the people I shared them with.

From my most recent travels with my dearest friends Milton Matoi, Lynne Kaneshiro, Masayo Moro, Leo Tanaka, Val Ford, Olelo Paʻa Ogawa, and Randy Ogata, to the most exciting fishing and hunting trips

My family and me at Kapiʻolani Community College for a Farm-to-Table event.

with Uncle Barton and Uncle Earl, and the great eating times from "small kid days" spent with Aunty Lynne and my cousin Brandyn Akamine, this book is a testament to the impact you have had on my life. I have been blessed by your love and kindness. Like this book, you are the "shining gems" that catch my heart!

Special thanks to longtime family friends Glen and Amy Shinsato for your friendship, support, and for the donation of the pork products used for the dishes and photos in this book.

Happy cooking!

Love,
Grant

The Hawai'i Cooks Series

This series is not meant to be a guide to the "traditional" cooking of any ethnic group. You can find those cookbooks in any bookstore. These books are a reflection of the various cuisines as they have developed—deliciously—in our islands.

There is a difference. Each immigrant group arrived here over a set period of years, with eating habits that reflected those of the homeland at that time. Back in Asia or Portugal, meanwhile, cuisine grew and changed. This evolution worked both ways. In Hawai'i, cooks adapted traditional dishes to local ingredients. And as circumstances improved, they used more of the sugar and meat that became affordable to them.

End result: Today a visitor from Japan might find our Japanese food recognizable but sweet; a Korean might be surprised by the amount of meat on the typical Korean menu; someone from Portugal might wonder, what is this thing we call Portuguese Bean Soup?

The heritage is to be respected, the differences to be celebrated, the deliciousness simply to be enjoyed.

The *Hawai'i Cooks* series includes Korean and Portuguese cuisines and will continue with Japanese, Chinese, and Filipino cuisines.

Dig in.

Betty Shimabukuro and Muriel Miura
Editors

Introduction

My grandmother described me as an inquisitive, quiet boy, hard-headed at times, but always distracted by colorful, shiny, beautiful things like fruits, flowers, and jewels. A picky but voracious eater, I would always over-indulge in the foods that I liked.

Grandma and I on the set of my cooking show, What's Cooking Hawai'i.

Forty-plus years later, I am the same. An obsessive-compulsive artist, one who sculpts and carves fruits and vegetables into beautiful flowers. A passionate instructor of culinary arts and culinary competition, always focused on the task at hand, yet still daydreaming about the future. I confess I can be temporarily blinded by the beauty of the culinary arts, from the prime fresh ingredients that inspire me to the exquisite dishware I collect to put the finishing touches on my work. These elements to me are like diamonds, sapphires, and emeralds—the jewels that captivated me in my youth.

I can honestly say that food rules my life. It is my daily motivator, drives me to work hard, and is the source of constant daydreams about what fantastic product I will encounter next.

I am locally born, raised, and educated; internationally trained and traveled. Traveling helps me stay in touch with my Okinawan soul, but my family here in Hawai'i keeps me grounded.

The recipes in this book represent a wide spectrum of good eating, from family versions of traditional favorites to my contemporary creations. I'd like to thank my mom, Candace Sakuda; stepdad, Karl Sakuda; sister, Kari Sakuda; and brother, Kelly Sakuda. They are the willing guinea pigs who helped me refine the recipes in this book, and also comprise the supportive family that allows me to be me.

Please enjoy the recipes, and happy cooking!

Roots of Ryukyuan Cuisine

The Kingdom of Okinawa benefits from its distance to Japan— far enough to maintain its own identity, yet close enough to forge common ties. The result is a culture and cuisine both colorful and rich in tradition, influenced not only by Japan but by contact with China and other parts of Asia.

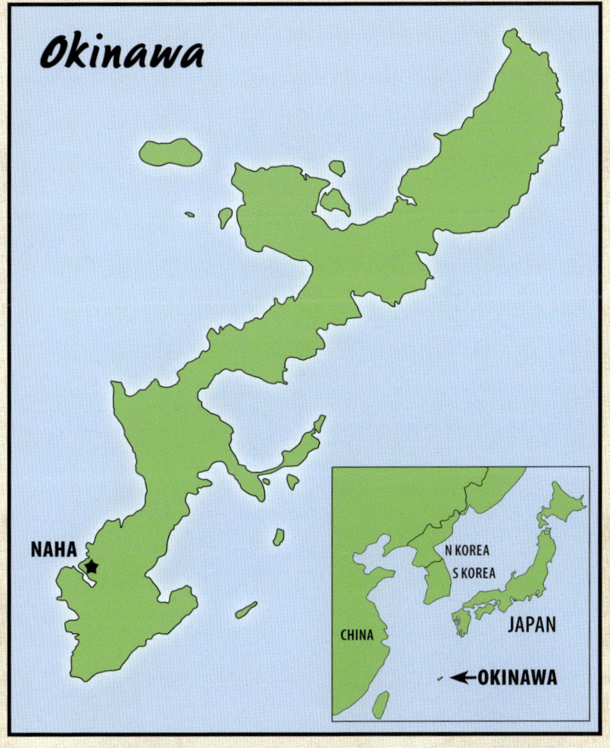

Ryukyuan, or Okinawan, cuisine has two origins: "Shuri cuisine" for the nobility, based on Japanese and Chinese traditions and tied to Shuri, the seat of Okinawan government in the 15th century; and "commoners' food" eaten by the masses.

Shuri cuisine centered on the subtle flavors of fine products, cut in a skillful manner, cooked and presented in a noble way. This included the use of fine lacquered, artistic ceramics, or fine carved wooden vessels. Perfection of this type of cuisine was a necessity in treating with the nobles of China and Japan.

The predominance of pork in the Okinawan diet is a key reflection of Chinese influence. The Japanese diet leaned more heavily on seafood, and Buddhism's vegetarian principals held greater sway. Even after Okinawa fell under Japanese rule in 1609, the preference for pork remained.

Further distinguishing Ryukyuan eating habits were the crops and grazing animals that flourished in the region. Sweet potato and bitter melon became staples of the diet. Local tastes also favored goat—it was even eaten raw as sashimi, a delicacy. Like pork, goat could easily be preserved, either stewed or braised in soy sauce and sugar to retard spoilage in the days before refrigeration.

Rafute (Okinawan Braised Sliced Pork Belly), see recipe on page 53.

Still, Japanese food notes are basic to Okinawan cooking. Dashi, the classic Japanese soup stock made from kelp and dried bonito flakes, for example, is key to most Okinawan soups and simmered dishes. Sweet-salty soy-based flavors are another shared trait of the two cuisines.

Dried bonito flakes used to make soup stock (dashi).

After World War II, the military on American bases introduced many previously unknown foods to a starving postwar population. Thus developed such early fusion dishes as champuru (stir-fry) made with Spam or hot dogs, and andagi-battered hot dogs eaten with ketchup like a corn dog.

One famous Okinawan dish, taco rice, reflects Latin influences. Steamed rice is topped with seasoned ground beef, diced tomatoes, shredded lettuce, cheese, olives, and pickled peppers in this funky fusion favorite.

The first Okinawan immigrants to Hawai'i, arriving as plantation workers at the dawn of the 1900s, were all commoners, so the food they created here was based on classic, rustic dishes. They substituted grown-in-Hawai'i ingredients for similar items unavailable outside of Okinawa.

This is the basis for the local-style Okinawan cuisine most of us in Hawai'i are familiar with. It is, in a way, caught in a time warp. Flavors are similar to what you would have found in Okinawa in the late 1800s—a heavy hand on the soy sauce and sugar, necessary back then to help preserve foods. At the same time, the food took on influences of the local culture, based on the sharing of ingredients and experiences with native Hawaiians and immigrants from Japan, Puerto Rico, Korea, the Philippines, and Portugal.

Today in Okinawa it is clear that the subtle flavors and refined techniques of Japanese cuisine have had a strong impact on chefs, who have learned to let the natural flavor of their ingredients shine. Much less soy sauce and sugar is used, as it is no longer needed to help preserve the food. The flavor of typical Okinawan dishes has become more refined and less bold.

But in modern Hawai'i, we still like that soy-sugar profile and no one is going to talk us out of it. This book certainly won't try to, although my hope is that you will follow me as I travel down some other flavor paths—Okinawan foods beyond rafute, champuru and andagi. Join me on an exploration of the richness and color of the Uchinanchu menu.

Grandma's Story: My Inspiration

I dedicate this book to my grandma, Jeanette Setsuko Akamine. A savvy business woman who always put other people first, she let her husband have the limelight, while being the backbone of the family and a quiet problem solver. She is my closest confidant, my life coach, and Okinawan mentor.

Jeanette was born in 1924 to Beiga Arashiro and Toshi Matsuda in Hukipu Camp, Kekaha Mauka Plantation, Kaua'i. My grandma and her family moved to Honolulu in 1938 after the passing of her mother.

The newly named "Arthur" Yonega Beiga Arashiro and his daughter began their new lives in the big city, facing a challenge they had never experienced on the plantation, discrimination for being Okinawan. My grandmother asked her father why the immigrants from mainland Japan looked down upon her and told her that they would never let their sons marry her—his simple answer: Just overlook it, hold your head high, and be a proud Okinawan.

Arashiro family at Myogaya Restaurant in 1949.

In 1940 Arthur married Fujiko Yogi and opened Myogaya Restaurant. A young Jeanette went to school, worked in the restaurant cooking Okinawan basics like andansu, pig's feet soup, champuru, and konbu maki, while helping raise her 10 younger siblings.

After graduating from Saint Francis High School, Jeanette married her first love, Bernard Seiso Akamine. A decorated World War II veteran of the "Go for Broke" 100th Infantry Battalion, Bernard was a proud American. He and Jeanette raised my aunt, my mom, and my uncle to be respectful, law-abiding citizens who spoke only English and ate a typical American diet—with one exception. On

Bernard and Jeanette Akamine (Grandpa and Grandma). Kekaha Mauka Plantation Camp (a.k.a. Hukipu Camp), Kaua'i, 1946.

My grandparents, Bernard and Jeanette Akamine, newly married, 1946.

New Years Day at his parents' Kahalu'u farm, traditional Okinawan and Japanese dishes were served.

As her children began their schooling, so did Jeanette. She learned cosmetology from Royal School of Beauty Culture in Honolulu, opening J's Waikiki Beauty Salon in 1964. Stints as president of the Honolulu Hairdressers and Cosmetologists Association and chairwoman of the Hawai'i State Hair Fashion Committee are highlights of her successful 40-year career.

The 1970s brought Jeanette and Bernard their first grandchildren and a renewed interest in finding their roots in Okinawa. They would indulge this interest for four decades

Grandma with former Honolulu mayor Frank Fasi, 1974.

through family trips to Okinawa and Brazil to meet relatives and experience the true Uchinanchu culture and cuisine.

Grandma and I still live together. She remains active, doing the things she loves, making sushi and jellies. She continues to inspire me with her strength, youthful appetite, fascination for the color purple, and her desire to experience new things while living life to the fullest. She is the reason I am who I am today.

Okinawan Basics

I have to admit that my love for eating tofu was enhanced by the ease at which I could prepare it. The five minutes it takes to cut open a container, cut, plate, and garnish the tofu is just a blink of an eye compared to the time and effort it takes to make it from scratch.

But it is only by making tofu yourself that you can fully appreciate the finished product and come to

continued on the next page

understand how the process creates many other ba-sic ingredients, such as tofu lees (okara) and dried soy bean sheets (yuba). I feel that such basic skills com-prise a dying art that needs to be taught to the young-er generation.

Many recipes in this book contain ingredients once commonly made from scratch, out of necessity. These items were time-consuming projects, due to the length of pickling times or the processing of raw ingredients. Today, thankfully, most of these ingredi-ents are commonly found in supermarkets, already made, and so much more convenient.

But if you have the time and energy to make these recipes from scratch, I encourage you to do so, as it will give you a greater appreciation for what we take for granted. You will also come to realize how much work was involved in putting food on the table for our grandparents and great-grandparents.

Other recipes in this chapter, while not "from-scratch" recipes, were at one time the building blocks of a tradi-tional plantation Okinawan meal. I hope this chapter brings you closer to the dish-es of your childhood, and returns you to the moment when happiness set in—din-ner time!

Gomae
Ground Sesame Seed Dressing for Vegetables

Yield: Dressing for ½ pound of blanched vegetables

This dressing is commonly used to flavor blanched beans or blanched spinach. Hard vegetables like carrots should be cut into thin strips before blanching and tossing in this dressing. Leafy greens should be blanched and squeezed to extract any liquid that may dilute the dressing.

Goma Dressing:

- 1 tablespoon toasted goma (sesame seeds)
- 1 tablespoon sugar
- 1 tablespoon dashi (Japanese broth)
- 1 teaspoon rice wine vinegar
- 1 tablespoon shoyu (soy sauce)

- ½ pound of your favorite blanched solid vegetables cut into ¼-inch thick strips
- 1 teaspoon salt
- 1 teaspoon toasted goma (sesame seeds)

Using a Japanese mortar and pestle (suribachi), grind goma 1 minute, then add sugar, dashi, vinegar, and soy sauce. Continue grinding another minute to combine ingredients.

Place blanched vegetables into a bowl; sprinkle with salt and toss lightly. Add gomae dressing and toss until vegetables are evenly coated. Serve chilled and garnished with a sprinkle of toasted goma.

Suribachi: Japanese ceramic mortar and pestle, featuring a ceramic bowl that has a ribbed or grooved lining and a wooden dowel or pestle

Contemporary Gomae

Yield: 2 portions

My twist on the classic sesame seed dressing can be made in a mini food processor or blender—add all the ingredients at once and blend well. Leafy greens such as watercress, mustard cabbage, and napa cabbage mix well with this dressing, just make sure to squeeze out any excess liquid.

    1 tablespoon goma (sesame seeds)
    1 tablespoon sugar
    1 tablespoon miso (white soy bean paste)
    2 tablespoons dashi (Japanese broth)
    1 teaspoon rice wine vinegar
    ½ teaspoon yuzu kosho (citrus pepper paste)
    1 teaspoon shoyu (soy sauce)

    ½ pound blanched nanohana
       (rape blossoms) or broc-
       colini spears
    1 teaspoon toasted goma
       (sesame seeds) as garnish

In a suribachi (Japanese mortar and pestle), grind goma for about a minute, then add sugar and miso and grind another minute. Add dashi, vinegar, yuzu kosho, and shoyu and stir until combined.

Place nanohana or broccolini into a bowl or sealable plastic bag, add dressing and mix or shake until just combined. Serve chilled and garnished with toasted goma.

Hirayachi
Chive Crêpes

Yield: 20 to 30 crêpes, depending on size

This crêpe is commonly filled with brown sugar or andansu (pork soy bean paste) and called "popo crêpes." Shima rakkyo (pickled scallions) is another common filling.

3 cups water
3 eggs
2½ cups flour
2 teaspoons baking powder
½ teaspoon salt
½ cup chives, chopped

Combine ingredients in a bowl and mix until no lumps remain.

Heat a small sauté pan on high and add a little oil. When oil lightly smokes, add ¼ cup of the batter and swirl it in the bottom of the pan so that it covers the bottom evenly. Cook 1 minute, then flip crêpe using a spatula or chopsticks. Cook another minute, then set aside to cool while cooking remaining crêpes.

Fill crêpes as desired. Crêpes may be stacked using paper towels or parchment to keep them from sticking together.

Hirayachi
Contemporary Chive Crêpe

Yield: 20 to 30 pieces

*T*his is my modern version of the chive crêpe. It is slightly sweeter and stronger in texture, so that it can be made thinner than the original. If you omit the chives, this batter can be made into dessert crêpes topped with sweet fillings.

- **3 cups water**
- **¼ cup sugar**
- **1 cup heavy cream**
- **3 cups flour**
- **4 whole eggs**
- **2 egg yolks**
- **¼ cup butter, melted**
- **½ cup chives, chopped**

Combine all ingredients except chives in a bowl and mix well. Strain the mixture if lumps form; fold in chives.

Heat a small non-stick pan on medium heat and spray with a cooking-oil spray such as Pam or Vegaline. Add 2 ounces (¼ cup) batter and swirl pan so that batter covers the entire bottom of the pan. Cook 1 minute.

Turn crêpe using a spatula and cook another minute (then set aside to cool while cooking remaining crêpes). Fill crêpes as desired.

Crêpes may be stacked, using paper towels or parchment to keep them from sticking together.

Jushi: Rice Reborn

Kanduba jushi, a rice gruel with sweet potato leaves, was a regular starch on the table when I was growing up, usually appearing a few days after the rice was cooked.

Grandma used a large rice cooker. We consumed the freshly cooked rice that evening, then refrigerated the leftovers, which were reheated in the microwave or made into kandaba jushi. We'd eat it until it was gone, then cook rice again. This was the routine in our three-person household for three decades, until Grandpa passed in 2012.

My grandmother Akamine and I posing in front of our Christmas tree, 1975.

The sweet potato leaves that we used grew quickly in our garden. It was my belief that my grandpa planted lots of sweet potato for my sake—I was a "picking menace" as a child, running into the yard and picking whatever caught my eye. I thought Grandpa was trying to appease my constant need to harvest, but later I found that my grandparents just really enjoyed their kanduba jushi. The actual potatoes, harvested months later, were a bonus.

Grandma believes that Okinawans live long, healthy lives because of their regular consumption of kanduba (sweet potato leaves), goya (bitter melon) and sannin (ginger).

Jushi
Okinawan Rice Gruel

Yield: 8 portions

This classic porridge was made from the rice that was scorched on the bottom of the pot (kama) or from leftover rice. Green leafy herbs—such as sweet potato leaves (kanduba), mugwort (fushiba), or Japanese parsley (mitsuba)—were commonly added for flavor and to give the dish medicinal properties

8 cups dashi (Japanese broth) or water
2 cups freshly cooked or day old medium- or short-grain rice
1 tablespoon salt
3 tablespoons shoyu (soy sauce)

Place the dashi or water in a pot and bring to a boil. Add rice and reduce heat to simmer. Cook, stirring frequently to keep the rice from sticking to the bottom of the pot, until rice is soft and liquid has thickened (30 to 45 minutes). Season with salt and shoyu.

Shisa, Okinawan statues that look like a cross between a lion and a dog, guard against evil and are often placed as pairs on rooftops or by entryways. Traditionally, when displayed in pairs, the shisa on the left has a closed mouth to keep good spirits in and the shisa on the right has an open mouth to scare bad spirits.

Kanduba Jushi
Grandma Jeanette Akamine's Okinawan Sweet Potato Leaf Rice Gruel

Yield: 8 portions

Grandma's kanduba jushi would last us several days. It is soup-like on the day it is prepared and becomes very thick and risotto-like the next day, even when reheated.

8 cups dashi (Japanese broth)
2 cups day-old cooked rice
2 slices ginger
2 tablespoons shoyu (soy sauce)
1 cup kanduba (sweet potato leaves)
¼ cup takuan (pickled turnip), chopped

Bring broth to boil in a medium pot. Add rice and ginger. Stir well and continue to cook over medium heat until rice is soft and liquid is thickened, about 30 minutes, stirring frequently to prevent rice from sticking to the bottom of the pot.

Season with shoyu and add kanduba. Stir another 3 to 5 minutes until the leaves are wilted. Serve in a bowl garnished with chopped takuan.

My grandmother Akamine taking me out for the first time to pick mangos— my first harvest.

Hawai'i Shima Jushi
Hawai'i Island Rice Gruel

*T*his is my contemporary version of classic rice gruel, influenced by ingredients grown on the Big Island.

8 cups dashi (Japanese broth)
3 small Big Island abalone
1½ cups freshly cooked or day old cooked rice
2 tablespoons kizami wasabi (pickled Japanese horseradish) stems and leaves
½ cup warabi (fiddlehead fern shoots), thinly sliced
¼ cup ogo (seaweed), chopped
1 teaspoon salt
¼ cup green onions, chopped

Place dashi and abalone in a medium pot and bring to a boil. Boil abalone 10 minutes, then remove and set aside to cool. Reduce heat to medium and add rice. Cook, stirring frequently, until rice softens, about 5 to 7 minutes.

Slice abalone and return it to the pot along with the kizami wasabi, warabi and chopped ogo. Stir well to combine and season with salt. Serve hot, garnished with chopped green onions.

Warabi (fiddlehead fern shoots)

I LOVE TOFU!

Yes, I am shouting. I have loved tofu in all its many forms for as long as I can remember. Silken tofu topped with grated ginger, chopped green onions, and soy sauce. Firm tofu diced and stir-fried, deep-fried and seasoned, served cold in a salad, or crumbled into shirae with other vegetables.

Tofu has many forms, but we always bought it, never making it from scratch. Only recently have I learned the art of tofu-making, and have come to realize the importance of the process. It is not just tofu that is created, but also yuba and okara, which make their way into other Okinawan dishes.

The first step in tofu making is to soak the dried soy beans in water for eight hours or overnight. The rehydrated beans are then ground into a mash and then boiled in the water that was used to soak the beans.

The cooked mixture is strained through a cheesecloth and the dried cooked particles of soy beans left in the cheesecloth are called okara. The liquid that drains through the cheesecloth is soy milk.

When the soy milk is brought to a boil, a thin skin forms on the surface—this is removed and dried to form yuba. The soy milk is then ready to be turned into tofu. This process can take hours and has really given me a true appreciation of those who take the time and effort to make this basic item from scratch.

Tofu
Basic Firm Soy Bean Curd
Yield: 1 pound block

The difference between a silken or soft tofu and firm tofu is the amount of nigari added to coagulate the soy milk. Nigari (magnesium chloride), derived from ocean water, is available for purchase in Japanese markets or online sites such as eBay or Amazon. A small amount of nigari will thicken the milk to form soft tofu, while a greater amount is needed to "curdle" the milk. Dried seeds or powders such as macha (green tea powder) or goma (sesame seeds) can be added to the simmering soy milk to create a flavored tofu.

3 cups dried soybeans
1 gallon water
1 teaspoon salt
1 tablespoon magnesium chloride or nigari (Japanese bitter coagulant)
2 tablespoons water

Soak soybeans in 1 gallon water at room temperature for a minimum of 8 hours, or overnight.

Strain water from the beans into a pot. Grind beans in a food processor until almost smooth and add to the soaking water in the pot. Bring to a simmer and cook 30 minutes. Add salt. Turn off heat and strain through a cheesecloth-lined strainer or colander (the liquid is soy milk; the solids are soybean lees, or okara).

Place strained soy milk into another pot and heat until simmering.

Dissolve nigari in 2 tablespoons water and add to simmering soy milk. Allow pillows of coagulated soy protein to form (about 2 minutes). Pour contents of pot through a clean cheesecloth-lined strainer to separate the liquid from the coagulated soy. Place the coagulated soy in a block mold and weigh it down for 10 minutes, then remove the firm block of tofu from the mold and store in cold water until ready to use.

Okara
Stir-Fried Tofu Lees

Yield: 8 portions

O*kara comprises the solids left after soybeans are cooked and strained to make tofu. It is a nutritious byproduct that can be combined with any number of ingredients to make a hearty main dish.*

2 tablespoons vegetable oil
¼ cup carrots, chopped
¼ cup green beans, chopped
¼ cup shiitake mushrooms or gobo (burdock root), julienne
½ cup konnyaku (gelatinous cake), chopped
½ cup aburage (deep-fried soybean curd), chopped
1 pound okara (tofu lees)
½ cup dashi (Japanese stock) or chicken stock
1 tablespoon sugar
1 tablespoon shoyu (soy sauce)
Black pepper, to taste
½ cup green onions, chopped

Place medium sauté pan over high heat; add oil. When oil lightly smokes, add all the chopped vegetables, konnyaku, and aburage; sauté 1 minute. Add okara. Deglaze with dashi or stock (loosen any bits stuck to bottom of pan). Stir well to incorporate liquid, then sprinkle with sugar. Add shoyu and black pepper stir until absorbed. Taste and adjust seasonings.

Add green onions and stir well. Serve hot or chill and serve cold. May be used to stuff an aburage cone to make a rice-free cone sushi.

Shirae
Crumbled Tofu Dressing

Yield: 6 portions

1 cup dashi (Japanese broth)
2 tablespoons mirin (sweet rice wine)
2 tablespoons shoyu (soy sauce)
1 tablespoon sugar
1 (10- to 12-ounce) block firm tofu
2 tablespoons toasted goma (sesame seeds), plus more for
   garnish

<u>Suggested blanched vegetables:</u>
Spinach
Watercress
Cabbage
Won Bok

Combine dashi, mirin, shoyu, and sugar in small saucepan; bring to a boil, stirring until sugar dissolves. Set aside.

Cut or break the tofu block into small pieces. Place in cheesecloth and squeeze to remove as much water as possible. Place in bowl and set aside.

Using a suribachi (Japanese mortar and pestle), grind goma for about one minute, then add to cooled broth mixture; grind another minute. Pour over tofu and mix well. Pour tofu mixture over one cup desired blanched vegetables; toss lightly and garnish with toasted goma. Serve immediately or chill before serving.

Sushi Gohan
Okinawan Vinegared Rice for Sushi

Yield: 3 cups

Okinawan sushi rice is slightly sweeter than the version we see in mainland Japan, mainly because food spoils very quickly in the warm climate of Okinawa. Additional sugar helps to reduce the PH-level of a food, making it more resistant to bacterial contamination.

- ¾ **cup rice wine vinegar**
- ½ **cup sugar**
- **1 teaspoon salt**
- **1 (5-inch) square piece dashi konbu (seasoned kelp)**
- **3 cups hot, freshly cooked white rice**

Place rice wine vinegar, sugar, salt, and dashi konbu in a small pot and stir until sugar is dissolved. Turn heat to high and bring to a boil. Remove the dashi konbu and let mixture cool to room temperature.

Drizzle vinegar mixture (su) over rice and gently fold or "cut" mixture into the rice while simultaneously fanning the rice (this helps it cool quickly and creates a shiny gloss on the surface of each grain). Use to make a variety of sushi (see page 126 and 129).

Shima Rakkyo
Okinawan Pickled Scallions

Yield: 24 portions

*S*hima rakkyo, Okinawan pickled scallion, is made with the green scallion stalk still attached, unlike mainland Japanese rakkyo, which is just the pickled white bulb. Shima rakkyo is commonly served in Okinawa with katsuoboshi (bonito flakes) and shoyu, and can also be enjoyed deep-fried or in hirayachi (chive crêpes).

2 pounds scallion bulbs with 3 to 5 inches of green stalk
2½ cups rice wine vinegar
7 ounces (1 cup) sugar
1 tablespoon salt

Wash the scallion bulbs well, dry them well, and place them in a glass jar or plastic container.

Place vinegar in a small pot and quickly bring to a boil. Add sugar and salt, stir until dissolved. Set aside to cool to room temperature.

Pour cooled vinegar mixture over scallions bulbs and chill for a minimum of 20 days. A 6-week pickling is best!

Shima rakkyo is a popular snack in Okinawa that can be fried, deep fried as tempura, or pickled. It's often served as the perfect accompaniment to beer or awamori in local izakayas.

Shirishiri
Fine Julienne Vegetable Stir Fry with Egg

Yield: 5 portions

*T*his is a favorite of home cooks in Okinawa. The term "shirishiri" refers to the thinness of the vegetables, usually cut with a slicer. This dish is commonly used as a filling for crêpes, although it may also be served as a vegetable side dish.

2 tablespoons vegetable oil
1 pound of your favorite firm vegetable (carrot, zucchini, jica-ma, eggplant, squash, or cabbage are great), fine julienne
2 eggs
2 tablespoons dashi (Japanese broth)
1 tablespoon shoyu (soy sauce)

Heat a wok or sauté pan on high; add oil. When oil lightly smokes add vegetables and sauté until limp. Add dashi and shoyu; stir well for 30 seconds. Turn heat to low and add eggs. Stir well, until eggs are cooked to desired doneness.

Goya

The Bitter Truth

Goya—commonly known as bitter melon, bitter gourd, or bitter squash—is a native of India but is enjoyed throughout the Asian continent, Southeast Asia, and the Western Pacific islands. High in vitamins and nutrients, goya is a folk remedy in many cultures, touted as a cure or pre-

continued on the next page

ventative for cancer, malaria, diabetes, chicken pox, measles, dysentery, colic, scabies—and is even used for weight loss.

Goya is believed to have come from Southeast Asia to Okinawa, where it has become symbolic of everyday cuisine. You will find thin slices in everything from salads to stir-fries to desserts.

Two main varieties are grown and sold in Hawai'i: The most common is the Chinese variety, distinguished by its long, cylindrical shape and relatively smooth, light green skin. This variety grows on a vine and is noted for its high yield. Its bitterness is a natural defense against bugs and critters and makes it relatively easy to grow. The second variety is the Indian. Commonly grown in Okinawa, this shorter, spikey-skinned, dark blue-green fruit is less bitter, and has a lower yield, making it harder to find.

Select goya with firm flesh and skin of uniform color. Look carefully for "bite marks"—dark perforations in the grooves of the skin—as they may indicate an internal worm. Goya should be refrigerated if not used immediately. Left at room temperature it will ripen. The flesh will become softer, turn from green to yellow to red, and become slightly sweet and extremely bitter.

The basic preparation for the fruit is to cut it in half lengthwise, scoop out all of the seeds, and carefully scrape away the internal pith, which contains a fair amount of bitterness. Sliced or diced goya can be soaked in slightly acidulated water (lemon water, for example) to help extract more bitterness (soaking in salted water enhances the bitterness). Goya can then be sautéed, steamed, stuffed, fried, or marinated.

No fear of frying

hrimp tempura was a favorite of my childhood. The fluffy cake-like yellow batter gave a slightly crunchy skin to the butterflied shrimp in the center. I was obsessed with it.

Little did I know, that type of tempura is the Okinawan version of the Japanese classic. As I became more traveled, I discovered the insanely crisp, straight Japanese ebi tempura. It was enjoyable to eat but felt strangely wrong.

Some have said that Okinawan immigrants in Hawai'i, feeling discrimination from those from mainland Japan, wanted to serve their own unique tempura. It was their way of saying, "I'm Uchinan-chu and Proud."

Fried foods are a favorite everywhere on the planet. Their crispy crunch is their charm, achieved through batter and breading.

Three main types of batter are common in Hawai'i: beer, Japanese-style, and Okinawan-style. All start with flour, one moistened with beer, the other two with water. The difference between Japanese and Okinawan batters is the addition of baking powder and yellow food coloring in the Okinawan.

Breading—a dry coating bound with beaten egg—was traditionally bread crumbs but can now be crushed or crumbled cereal, potato chips, or various "arare" crackers.

Regardless of the batter or breading, the success of frying tempura depends on oil temperature and the length of time the product fries in the oil. Tempura cooked too long at too low of a temperature will be greasy, tempura cooked too quickly at too high temperature could be scorched or undercooked in the center. The ideal oil temperature is 325 to 350°F. Assessing doneness is a tricky thing—the only way to guarantee your tempura cooks evenly is to slice the items you are frying to a thickness that will cook in a relatively short time, five minutes at the longest.

Goya Tempura
Beer-Battered Bitter Melon

Yield: 5 portions

Because this batter is thinner than the traditional, the tempura is fried very quickly in hot oil so that it crisps up quickly.

2 goya (bitter melon), cut into ¼-inch thick rings, seeds removed (see page 24)
¼ cup cornstarch
2 cups all-purpose flour
2½ cups of your favorite beer
1 egg
2 tablespoons of your favorite furikake (dried seasoned seaweed)
1 teaspoon salt
Vegetable oil, for deep-frying

Pat goya rings dry with paper towels then dust goya rings with cornstarch and set aside. To make batter, combine remaining ingredients in a bowl; whisk until smooth

Heat oil to 350°F. Dip goya rings in batter and deep-fry for about 2 minutes, or until golden brown; drain on absorbent paper. Serve hot.

Goya Nu Agimun or Goya Tempura
Batter Fried Bitter Melon

Yield: 5 portions

This Okinawan-style batter is thicker than most Japanese tempura batters, so medium-hot oil is used in frying. A longer frying time is needed to form a puffy, crispy skin. If the oil is too hot, the batter will brown quickly, yet remain raw inside. If you are pre-soaking your goya in acidulated water to remove some bitterness, make sure to pat it completely dry on paper towels before dusting it with flour.

2 whole goya (bitter melon), cut into ¼-inch thick slices, seeds removed (see page 24)
¼ cup flour

Batter:
2 cups flour
½ cup water
3 eggs
2 teaspoons salt
1 tablespoon sugar
1 teaspoon baking powder
2 drops yellow food coloring, optional

Vegetable oil for deep-frying

Pat goya rings dry with paper towels. Dust the goya rings with the flour; set aside. Whisk together remaining ingredients (except oil) in a bowl to make batter.

Heat oil to 320°F. Dip goya rings into batter (taking care to space out the rings) and deep-fry until golden brown. Place in a pan lined with paper towels to absorb any excess oil.

Goya ni Numun
Bitter Melon Braised in Miso Broth

Yield: 5 portions

*U*nlike champuru, in which the goya is quickly crisp-cooked, this dish gives it a long simmer, to emerge soft and infused with the flavors of miso and mirin.

2 tablespoons vegetable oil
2 goya (bitter melon)
1 teaspoon salt
2 cups pork stock or dashi (Japanese broth)
2 tablespoons shiro miso (white soy bean paste)
2 tablespoons mirin (sweet rice wine)
4 pieces aburage (deep-fried bean curd), cut in halves
2 eggs

Cut goya in half lengthwise; remove seeds and pith. Cut crosswise into ¾-inch-thick pieces and sprinkle with salt. Set aside 20 minutes, then rinse off excess salt or liquid and pat dry with paper towels.

Heat a wok on high and add oil. When oil lightly smokes, add goya and stir-fry 1 minute. Add dashi, miso, and mirin; stir well to dissolve miso. Add aburage. Reduce heat and simmer until goya is soft. Stir in eggs. As soon as eggs firm up turn off heat. Serve hot.

Champuru, a true champion

Goya Champuru—a traditional stir-fry of bitter melon, tofu and eggs—is the most familiar Okinawan dish to Americans. It has been a favorite in our house, in many forms and variations, for as long as I can remember.

Grandpa liked his with firm tofu, seasoned only with salt and pepper. He said that because he grew up poor on the plantations, salt and pepper were the only seasonings his family had. Soy sauce and sugar were expensive commodities reserved for very special occasions. Grandma remembers champuru with pork, goya, egg, and firm tofu, seasoned with salt and pepper. Like Grandpa, she said salt was used over soy sauce as it was more plentiful, but because her family raised chickens and pigs they had the luxury of pork and eggs.

I never really liked goya in any way until I became an adult. I now enjoy its bitter bite and I like my champuru seasoned with tsuyu (Japanese broth concentrate) to harmonize the goya's bitterness with the richness of the pork and the subtle softness of the tofu.

Goya Champuru
Stir-Fried Bitter Melon with Tofu

Yield: 5 portions

The key to this simple dish is to drain the tofu well before adding it to the wok or pan. Wet tofu will leach water and you will end up "boiling" the ingredients instead of searing them. If you choose not to use pork, a small amount of vegetable oil will be needed to sauté the bitter melon. It should be slightly charred to give off a smoky rich flavor. In Okinawa, Spam is sometimes used in place of pork to create a savory salty champuru.

½ pound pork belly, cut into ¼-inch thick slices

2 cups goya (bitter melon), cut into ¼-inch thick slices (see page 24)

1 (10- to 12-ounce) block firm tofu

1 teaspoon salt

2 eggs

Heat a wok on medium heat and add pork belly. Stir-fry until fat is rendered, then turn heat to high. Add goya and quickly stir-fry about 1 minute, then take a spoon and scoop bite-sized pieces of tofu from the block directly into wok. Stir-fry another minute, being careful not to break tofu. Season with salt.

Move mixture to back of the wok and add eggs; lightly scramble. Toss eggs with the rest of the ingredients and serve hot.

Goya Champuru
Contemporary Stir-Fried Bitter Melon with Tofu

Yield: 6 portions

My modern version of the classic.

2 tablespoons vegetable oil
2 cups goya (bitter melon), cut into ¼-inch thick slices (see
  page 24)
1 cup sweet onion, cut into ¼-inch thick slices
½ cup fresh or rehydrated dried wood ear mushroom (pepeau)
½ cup string beans, cut into 2-inch lengths
1 (10- to 12-ounce) block of your favorite firm tofu
½ cup dashi (Japanese broth)
1 tablespoon shoyu (soy sauce)
1 teaspoon oyster sauce
2 eggs
2 tablespoons green onions, chopped

Heat a wok on high and add oil. When oil lightly smokes add goya and onion; stir-fry about a minute. Add pepeau and string beans; stir-fry another minute. Using a spoon, scoop bite-sized chunks of tofu into the wok; toss lightly.

Add dashi and deglaze the wok (scrape up any bits stuck to the bottom); add shoyu and oyster sauce. Toss lightly, being careful not to break up the tofu.

Add eggs and toss until fully cooked. Serve hot in a bowl, garnished with the chopped green onion.

Goya Namashi
Pickled Bitter Melon Salad

Yield: 5 portions

his is the Okinawan version of the pickled cucumber and radish dish called namasu in mainland Japan. If the bitter melon flavor is too strong, decrease the amount and substitute cucumber to create a milder namashi. Other vegetables such as thin slices of green papaya, jicama, or carrots may also be added. Cooked seafood such as sliced cooked tako legs (octopus) are common mix-ins. Marinating ingredients in a sealed plastic bag can save space over a bulky bowl or other container.

¼ cup rice wine vinegar
¼ cup sugar
½ teaspoon salt
1 teaspoon ginger, grated
1 cup goya (bitter melon), cut in half crosswise, remove seeds and slice into ¼-inch-thick ringlets (see page 24)
½ cup carrots, thinly sliced
½ cup daikon (long radish), thinly sliced
Pinch of goma (sesame seeds) as garnish

Combine rice wine vinegar, sugar, salt, and ginger in a bowl and mix until sugar is dissolved. Add goya, carrots, and daikon; marinate a minimum of 2 hours. Chill before serving (may be held chilled for up to 1 week).

To serve, drain excess liquid and place in a bowl; garnish with toasted goma.

Goya Gomae
Bitter Melon Salad with Ground Sesame Seed Dressing

Yield: 5 portions

This is a favorite side dish in Okinawan bars. The bacon gives the dish a savory, salty flavor. In Okinawa, Spam and salt pork belly may be used when bacon is unavailable.

2 pieces bacon, cut into ¼-inch strips
2 cups goya (bitter melon), sliced crosswise ¼-inch thick (see page 24)
2 tablespoons toasted goma (sesame seeds)
1 teaspoon sugar
¼ cup dashi (Japanese broth)
1 teaspoon tsuyu (Japanese broth concentrate)

Sauté bacon in a pan over high heat and add goya. Lightly singe both; set aside in a bowl to cool.

Place goma, sugar, dashi, and tsuyu in a mini food processor and blend until smooth. Pour the sesame dressing over bacon and goya; toss well. Serve warm or chilled.

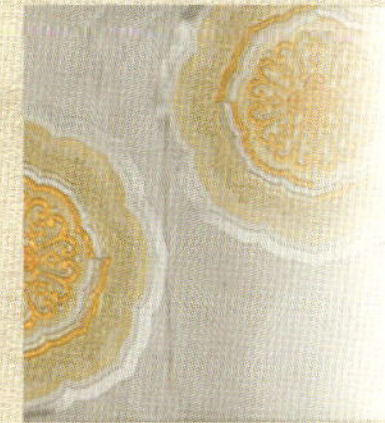

The art of making glassware in Okinawa changed after WWII. There was a shortage of material, so local craftsmen began collecting discarded bottles from US troops. The glass was melted down, re-blown and shaped into colorful pieces. Okinawan glassware continues to be a prized tradition and industry.

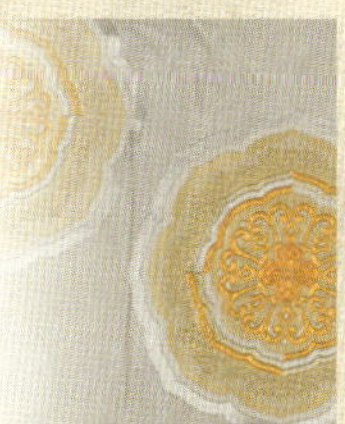

Yasei Namashi
Pickled Bitter Melon Salad with Seaweed

Yield: 4 portions

My modern version of the classic.

Marinade:
6 tablespoons rice wine vinegar
6 tablespoons sugar
1 teaspoon salt
2 teaspoons grated ginger

Salad:
½ cup goya (bitter melon), seeds removed and thinly sliced (see page XX)
½ cup cucumber, thinly sliced
¼ cup jicama, thinly sliced
¼ cup green papaya, thinly sliced
¼ cup warabi (fiddle head ferns), thinly sliced
¼ cup carrot, thinly sliced
½ cup ogo or wakame (seaweed), cut into 1-inch lengths

Start by combining the marinade ingredients in a bowl and mix until sugar is dissolved. Add the salad ingredients and marinate at least 4 hours. Store chilled up to 1 week.

Notes: There is a greater amount of seasoning in relation to vegetables in this recipe due to the high water content of the vegetables used. The level of the marinade may not cover the surface of the vegetables, but as the vegetables marinate they will release a good amount of water, yielding enough liquid to cover the vegetables. Use a Ziplock bag for easier storage, if desired, instead of a bulky bowl or container.

Goya Namashi to Tako
Pickled Bitter Melon with Cooked Octopus

Yield: 4 portions

Marinade:
- 6 tablespoons rice wine vinegar
- 6 tablespoons sugar
- 1 teaspoon salt
- 2 teaspoons grated ginger

Salad:
- ½ cup goya (bitter melon), thinly sliced
- ½ cup cucumber, thinly sliced
- ½ cup cooked tako (octopus), thinly sliced
- ½ cup sweet onion, thinly sliced
- ½ cup ogo or wakame (seaweed), cut into 1-inch lengths

Combine the rice wine vinegar, sugar, salt, and ginger in a bowl and mix until the sugar dissolves completely.

Add remaining ingredients and marinate for a minimum of 4 hours. Store chilled until ready to serve. May be held chilled for up to 1 week.

Pork

Primary Protein

Pork is the main protein in Okinawan cuisine, the basis of many of its best-known dishes—rafute (braised pork belly) and pig's feet soup.

Pork also represents perhaps the greatest bond between Hawai'i and Okinawa, dating to the post-World War II years, when many in the homeland were starving. In

continued on the next page

1948, a group of seven Okinawans in Hawai'i rallied the local community, collecting about $50,000 to purchase 550 pigs from a farm in Oregon, then traveling with the animals via a military transport ship to Okinawa.

This humanitarian act provided not just immediate sustenance for the Okinawan people, but the basis for their recovery as the animals reproduced.

In 2011, descendants of those seven men were honored at the Worldwide Uchinanchu Festival in Naha City. The festival committee, quoted in the Okinawan newspaper *Ryukyu Shimpo*, said: "We consider their achievements to be an essential piece of the history of the Worldwide Uchinanchu network. We must not let this be watered down by the passage of time."

The Okinawan diet makes use of all parts of the pig, from the ears to the feet. In discussions of Okinawan food it is often said, "every part of a pig can be eaten except its hooves and its oink."

This love of pork reflects the influence of China more than Japan, where fish is more common at the table. When a pig was slaughtered, the meat could be preserved in many ways:

> Meat was heavily salted and stored in ceramic jars (masu gami) or wrapped in straw and hung to dry.
>
> Miso was used to pack meat in ceramic jars to ferment (misu gami).
>
> Fatty parts were cooked down to render the fat, which was collected and held in ceramic jars (anda gami). The cooked skin or meat was cooked again with miso, sugar, and ginger to create anda insu or andansu.

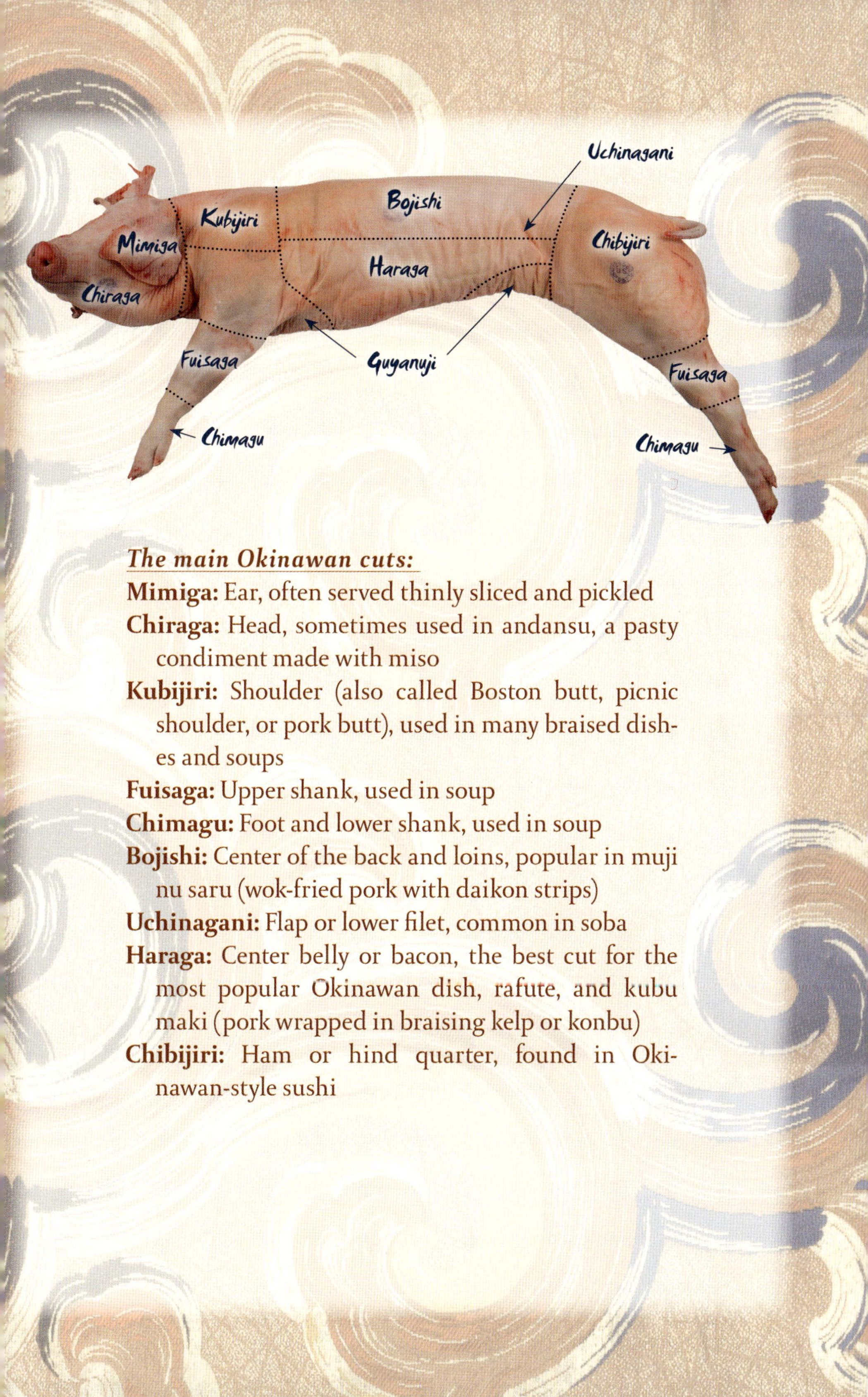

The main Okinawan cuts:

Mimiga: Ear, often served thinly sliced and pickled

Chiraga: Head, sometimes used in andansu, a pasty condiment made with miso

Kubijiri: Shoulder (also called Boston butt, picnic shoulder, or pork butt), used in many braised dishes and soups

Fuisaga: Upper shank, used in soup

Chimagu: Foot and lower shank, used in soup

Bojishi: Center of the back and loins, popular in muji nu saru (wok-fried pork with daikon strips)

Uchinagani: Flap or lower filet, common in soba

Haraga: Center belly or bacon, the best cut for the most popular Okinawan dish, rafute, and kubu maki (pork wrapped in braising kelp or konbu)

Chibijiri: Ham or hind quarter, found in Okinawan-style sushi

Mimiga
Marinated Pig's Ear

Yield: 8 portions

*P*igs' ear is a favorite snack or "bar food" in Okinawa. Ears are boiled or grilled whole, then cut into thin strips and simmered again in soy sauce, sugar, and ginger or pickled with vinegar and chilies. It may also be eaten in a peanut-based sauce similar to Indonesian satay sauce. Locally, pig's ears can be bought in Chinatown and usually take about 45 minutes to cook when boiled.

Recipe #1:
    1 tablespoon garlic, minced
    1 teaspoon chili pepper, minced
    2 tablespoons vinegar or ponzu (citrus soy sauce)
    1½ tablespoons shoyu (soy sauce) plus ½ tablespoon lime juice
    1 cup pig's ear, boiled or grilled and julienned

Place all ingredients in a bowl and toss well. Serve immediately or chill for a few hours and serve it cold.

Recipe #2:
    ½ cup dashi (Japanese broth) or chicken broth
    2 tablespoons shoyu (soy sauce)
    2 tablespoons sugar
    1 tablespoon ginger, grated
    1 cup pig's ear, boiled or grilled and julienned

Place dashi, shoyu, sugar, and ginger in a small pot and bring to a boil. Add pig's ears and simmer until the liquid reduces by half. Remove pig's ears from liquid and serve.

Kubu Irichi
Simmered Sliced Pork, Tofu, and Seaweed

Yield: 5 portions

*T*his is a comfort dish—a stew of pork belly and tofu spiked with a bit of rice wine.

1 (10- to 12-ounce) block firm tofu
2 tablespoons vegetable oil
1 pound pork belly
4 cups water
1 (9-ounce) block konnyaku (lily bud jelly), cut ¼-inch thick
6 strips of nishime konbu (thin kelp)
1 cup kamaboko (fishcake), julienned
2 tablespoons shoyu (soy sauce)
2 tablespoons awamori (Okinawan rice wine) or sake
1 tablespoon sugar

Cut tofu into ¼-inch-thick slices; dry on paper towel. Heat sauté pan on high and add oil. Sear tofu slices to a golden brown; set aside on paper towels to absorb excess oil.

Place pork belly and water in small pot and boil 15 minutes to render fat. Remove pork from liquid and cut into ¼-inch-thick strips; set liquid aside.

Cut fried tofu and konnyaku into ¼-inch-thick strips. Rehydrate konbu and cut into ¼-inch-thick strips.

Place 1 cup of reserved pork liquid in sauté pan or wok on high; quickly bring to boil. Add konbu, pork, tofu, and fishcake. Stir well and season with shoyu, awamori or sake, and sugar, stirring until sugar is dissolved. Simmer 5 minutes, or until liquid is reduced by half. Serve hot.

The classic condiment: Andansu

A traditional paste made from pork, sugar, miso, and ginger, this room-temperature staple is the center of every Okinawan meal. Served as a topping on rice balls (musubi), or a flavorful filling in crêpes, or even as a dipping sauce for raw vegetables, andansu is as Okinawan as you can get.

My grandfather told an interesting story of the lunch he carried to Washington Intermediate School in the early 1930s. The eldest son of immigrant farmers, his daily lunch was a small musubi with about a teaspoon of andansu smeared on it. My great grandmother, Kame Akamine, made andasu from the skin and fatty off-cuts of pork, which resulted in a smooth fatty paste. Because the family was poor, those were the only cuts of pork she could trade for her homegrown vegetables.

My great-grandmother and I in Okinawa, January 1, 1974.

The teachers at Washington Intermediate insisted that Grandpa's lunch was in no way adequately nutritious for a growing boy. They insisted that he buy a two-cent bowl of soup to eat with his andansu-flavored musubi, but he didn't, as the family could not afford even that two cents a day.

My grandma grew up raising chickens and pigs and the andansu she learned to make was made from meatier cuts of pork. This resulted in an andansu with shredded pieces of meat.

Regardless of the type of pork used, the process of making andasu is long, but the result is a cherished condiment that can be enjoyed at every meal!

Anda Insu or Andansu
Rendered Pork Miso Paste

Yield: 8 portions

After a pig was slaughtered, the skin and fatty off-cuts were boiled to break down the tissues. Sugar, miso, and ginger were added, and the mixture continued to cook until a thick paste formed. The paste was held in ceramic jars or containers at room temperature, thus this was a means of preserving the pork for a long period. This condiment is used to flavor rice or crêpes. Andansu remains a favorite to this day.

- **2 cups water**
- **1 pound fatty pork belly, cut into thin slices or ground in a food processor**
- **1 tablespoon ginger, grated**
- **½ cup shiro miso (white soy bean paste)**
- **½ cup sugar**
- **½ cup mirin (optional, if a sweeter andansu is desired)**

Place the water and pork in a medium-sized pot over medium heat; simmer 45 minutes to completely render fat. Add miso, ginger, sugar, and mirin, if using, and stir well, until sugar dissolves. Reduce heat to low and continue to simmer while stirring occasionally until a thick paste forms. Store chilled.

Among Okinawa's many traditional arts is its pottery—Tsuboya—which originated back before the 17th century, when the Ryukyu kingdom centralized the industry in one area, Naha city. You can still find many galleries and stores selling these beautiful crafts—from intricately painted dish ware to statues.

Tofu Tu Nasubi Unbushi
Stir-Fried Tofu, Eggplant and Pork

Yield: 5 portions

Tofu and eggplant act as a blank canvas in this dish, absorbing the vibrant flavors of miso, garlic, and ginger.

2 tablespoons vegetable oil
1 pound pork shoulder, cut into thin strips about 2 inches long, 1-inch wide and ⅓-inch thick
1 (10- to 12-ounce) block firm tofu, cut into 1-inch cubes
1 long eggplant, cut into 1-inch cubes
1 cup dashi (Japanese broth) or chicken stock
2 tablespoons shiro miso (white soy bean paste)
1 teaspoon salt
½ cup green onions, cut into 1-inch lengths
1 teaspoon garlic, grated
1 teaspoon ginger, grated

Heat a wok or sauté pan on high and add oil. When oil lightly smokes add pork; sauté 2 minutes. Add tofu and eggplant; deglaze with stock (scrape up any bits stuck to bottom of pan). Gently stir in miso until dissolved. Season with salt; add green onion, ginger, and garlic. Simmer another 2 minutes, or until eggplant flesh is soft and skin is wrinkled.

Rafute: The Belly is the Best

Pork belly and pork shoulder are the main cuts used to make rafute, one of the most widely recognized and loved Okinawan dishes. The belly is best, as the layers of fat and meat produce a very tender and moist result, with the skin retaining the dark, rich color of the braising liquid and adding visual appeal.

Pork shoulder is more commonly used today, as it is meatier with less fat and is easily found in local markets, fresh or frozen. The only downfall to using the shoulder is that it has no skin and therefore will not produce a shiny surface like the skin of the pork belly. To make rafute, the pork is cut into logs which are boiled in water to remove excess fat. Traditionally, this fat was collected and allowed to solidify for use like a cooking oil.

The semi-tender, partially cooked logs of pork are sliced and simmered in soy sauce, sugar, ginger, and sake or awamori (Okinawan rice liquor) until the reduced braising liquid glazes the surface of the slices. This was not only a means to flavor the slices but also to help preserve the pork slices in the days prior to refrigeration.

The thickened braising liquid was used to flavor other dishes, such as champuru, or diluted with water or dashi and used to braise fish collars (kama), split fish heads or even tuna eyes. The term for this style of braising is nitsuke.

Okinawan Braised Sliced Pork Belly

Yield: 8 portions

While time consuming, this ultimate Okinawan pork dish is well worth the effort. The pork slices are served without the braising liquid, but the liquid should be saved as it is the base for sauces served with many other dishes. Chill the liquid so the fat solidifies and can be removed, then the liquid can be heated as a "defatted" sauce.

3 pounds pork belly
½ gallon water or as needed
2 cups dashi (Japanese broth) or pork stock
1 cup awamori (Okinawan rice wine) or sake
¼ cup shoyu (soy sauce)
2 tablespoons shiro miso (white soy bean paste)
¼ cup sugar
1 clove garlic, crushed
1 piece ginger, sliced ¼-inch thick

Place pork belly in large pot and add water to cover. Turn heat to high and bring to a boil. Reduce heat to medium and cook, covered, or until skin is tender, 30 to 40 minutes. Remove pork from pot and set aside to cool. Remove fat from remaining pork stock. This liquid can be used in place of dashi to finish the dish.

Once pork has cooled enough to handle, slice into ½-inch-thick slices. Place dashi, awamori or sake, shoyu, miso, sugar, garlic, and ginger in large sauté pan or shallow brazier and quickly bring to a boil, making sure sugar is dissolved. Reduce to simmer and add sliced pork in neat, even rows. Simmer until liquid reduces by three-quarters (about another 30 minutes).

Serve slices of rafute without remaining sauce as the pork should be highly flavored from the long simmering process.

Note: The pork can be cut into 2-inch squares instead of slices, and then simmered in the braising liquid until the liquid is reduced by three-quarters. This is a more traditional method.

Pork and Taro Stem Miso-Flavor Soup

Yield: 5 portions

The stem of a plant in the taro family called zuiki is featured in this soup. Loofa gourd (hechima) or long squash (hyotan) are great substitutes. This very simple soup allows you to fully enjoy the flavor of the pork.

1 pound pork shoulder
8 cups water
4 cups pork stock or dashi (Japanese broth)
½ cup shiro miso (white soy bean paste)
1 pound zuiki (thick taro stalks)
1 (10- to 12-ounce) block firm tofu
Salt as needed

Place pork shoulder in a medium-sized pot with water and bring to a boil. Continue boiling for 30 minutes. Remove pork shoulder and cut into 1-inch cubes.

Skim fat from remaining liquid and add dashi or pork stock. Bring to boil and add miso, stirring until dissolved. Add cubed pork, zuiki, and tofu; simmer for additional 10 minutes. Season with salt, if needed.

Feet First

It's funny how we relate memories. For example, I associate pigs' feet soup with burning weeds.

My grandpa was very dedicated to his yard and driveway, so much so that we regularly got rid of the thin blades of grass that grew in the cracks of our driveway and surrounding

Grandpa and I, 1975.

sidewalks and curbs. Many little weeds grew in those cracks, especially a few weeks after a big rain.

Grandpa would light his handheld torch, then grab my hand and walk me around as he burned the weeds. I loved the way the weeds disappeared as they were torched. It was magical! I associated the sound of the torch with fun, and got excited every time I heard him light it.

As I grew older, I was allowed to torch the weeds myself. And after I proved I was able to responsibly handle the torch, I was allowed to singe the hairs off the pig trotters. This was not as much fun because the burning hairs smelled bad, but the soup Grandpa made from those trotters was amazing: the thick, savory, gelatinous broth tinged with ginger and cilantro, the soft squash, the spicy mustard cabbage, and the only thing I didn't care for, the peanuts.

To this day, when I shop for pig trotters or make pig's feet soup, I flash back to those good old days of torching weeds in our driveway. I guess it was a magical time!

Ashi Tebichi
Pig's Feet Soup

Yield: 5 portions

This dish is quite a production, what with the cleaning, long simmering and skimming, but the soup's warm goodness is worth the effort.

3 to 4 pounds pig's hoof and lower shank (trotters)
1 tablespoon sea salt
1 gallon water
5 (¼-inch-thick) slices ginger
1 thin strip nishime konbu (kelp)
4 dried shiitake mushrooms
1 large daikon (long radish) cut into 1½-inch cubes
3 tablespoons shoyu (soy sauce)
2 tablespoons awamori (Okinawan rice wine) or sake
1 cup karashina (mustard cabbage) leaves and stems, large dice
2 cups hyotan (long squash), large dice
Cilantro sprigs, for garnish (optional)
Grated ginger, for garnish (optional)

Clean pig's feet and shank well, making sure to remove any hairs (they can be torched or burnt off). Rub pig's feet with sea salt; let sit 15 minutes.

Place water in a large pot and quickly bring to a boil. Add salted pig's feet and ginger; let water return to boil. Reduce heat to low and simmer 1 hour, occasionally skimming fat from surface of pot.

Rehydrate konbu and shiitake mushrooms at same time. Tie konbu into knots 2 inches apart, then cut between knots. Cut shiitake mushrooms into quarters.

When pig's feet are tender, add konbu, shiitake mushrooms, daikon, and season with shoyu and awamori or sake. When mushrooms and konbu are tender, add mustard cabbage and squash; simmer 5 minutes. Garnish with cilantro and grated ginger as desired. Season with additional salt if needed.

Sokibuni No Shimun
Pork Spare Rib Soup

Yield: 5 portions

This is a very simple and basic pork rib soup. Add other ingredients, if desired, such as shiitake mushrooms, carrots, bell peppers, and zucchini.

1½ to 2 pounds St. Louis-style pork spare ribs
1 gallon water
3 strips nishime konbu (thin kelp)
1 cup daikon (long radish), large dice
½ cup shiro miso (white soy bean paste)
1 tablespoon grated ginger
1 cup karashina (mustard cabbage), leaves and stems, large-diced
3 tablespoons shoyu (soy sauce)

Rehydrate konbu and tie each strip into knots 2 inches apart; cutting between knots.

Cut pork into individual riblets; place in pot with water on high heat and bring to boil. Boil 30 minutes, occasionally skimming fat and scum from surface of water. Add konbu, daikon, miso, and grated ginger; simmer 15 minutes. Add karashina and shoyu. Serve immediately. Season soup with salt, if needed.

Nakami Nu Shimun
Pork Tripe Soup

Yield: 5 portions

This very simple soup may be augmented with vegetables. Long squash (hyotan), mustard cabbage, or thin strips of green papaya are recommended.

1 pound pork tripe
2 tablespoons rock salt
8 cups water
1 tablespoon ginger, grated
5 cups dashi (Japanese stock)
1 tablespoon shoyu (soy sauce)
2 hihatsu (Okinawan chili peppers), cut into thin strips

Place tripe in a bowl and sprinkle with rock salt. Rub salt into tripe to clean it. Rinse tripe, then cut it into thin 3-inch by ¼-inch strips. Place tripe into a medium-sized pot with water and ginger; quickly bring to boil. Boil 15 minutes, then drain, discarding liquid.

Place dashi into medium-sized pot; quickly bring to boil. Add tripe and reduce heat to simmer; add shoyu and hihatsu. Serve immediately. Season with additional salt, if needed.

Shishi Gobo Maki
Pork-Wrapped Burdock

Yield: 8 pieces

*T*his dish is like an inside-out kubu maki, in that the pork becomes the wrapper and the vegetables are the filling. If you cannot find good thick pieces of pork belly, you can use pork shoulder or even thick strips of bacon.

1 pound pork belly, sliced into 8 thin sheets, about 3-inches square
2 cups gobo (burdock root), julienned
1 cup carrots, julienned
8 strips kampyo (dried gourd strips), 8 inches long
6 cups dashi (Japanese broth) or chicken stock
1 cup awamori (Okinawan rice wine) or sake
3 tablespoons shoyu (soy sauce)
2 tablespoons sugar
1 thin slice ginger

Place a pork belly square on cutting board. At one end, place ⅛ of the gobo and carrot; roll up pork. Tie roll with kampyo. Repeat to make 8 rolls.

Place rolls in a medium-sized pot and cover with dashi. Turn heat to low and add awamori or sake, shoyu, sugar, and ginger; simmer 30 minutes. Serve hot or at room temperature.

Awamori, made from distilled long-grain rice, is indigenous to Okinawa. The process by which it's fermented and then distilled allows it to be made year-round despite Okinawa's hot climate. When shopping for awamori, ask for kusu, which is aged awamori. Enjoy it straight, on the rocks, or as one does in Okinawa—with water and ice.

All Wrapped Up

Kubu maki is a dish I always helped Grandma make when I was a child, but usually only once a year, on New Year's Eve.

She would cut and prepare the strips of pork belly, gobo, sometimes carrots, kampyo, and the konbu. Then she'd sit me down and show me how to wrap and tie each roll. This was her way of keeping me busy while she prepared her sushi ingredients.

The maki would be simmered early on New Year's Day, then we would pack the van with tons of food and head out to my great-grandparents' farm in Kahalu'u.

I loved that farm so much—not only because of the food or family, but because there were so many things to harvest and pick. I guess you can tell what kind of kid I was!

Eating the kubu maki was so enjoyable—the soft, salty, sweet, savory pork; the earthy, tender gobo; all held together with beautiful, smooth, shiny konbu. My grandmother praised me for wrapping them so well. "Good job rolling the kubu maki, Grant; our family will stay together this year like your kubu maki."

Those words went over my young head then, but stick in my heart today.

Now when I make kubu maki, I cut all of the ingredients and Grandma wraps them, symbolically holding the family together as she does so. She still oversees the simmering of these symbolic rolls: "Make sure the heat is just hot enough to cook the ingredients but not hot enough to cause the konbu to wrinkle or bubble." Or, "The outside appearance is just as important as the taste."

We eat kubu maki any time of the year now, but the time spent making it is always a special occasion.

Kubu Maki
Simmered Kelp-Wrapped Pork and Burdock

This dish that symbolizes family unity is commonly eaten year round, although it is a New Year's celebration standard. Colorful firm vegetables like carrots and string beans can be added as long as they are cut into strips of the appropriate length.

8 (8-inch) pieces nishime konbu (braising kelp)
½ pound pork belly, cut into ½-inch-by-3-inch strips
8 strips gobo (burdock root), ½-inch-by-3-inches
8 pieces kampyo (dried gourd strips), 8 inches long
6 cups dashi (Japanese broth)
3 tablespoons shoyu (soy sauce)
2 tablespoons sugar
1 thin slice ginger

Place 1 nishime konbu strip on a cutting board; place 1 piece of pork and 1 piece of gobo at one end. Roll until all of the konbu is used. Wrap 1 piece kampyo around the center of the roll, then tie in a knot. Repeat to make 8 rolls.

Place dashi in a medium-sized pot; quickly bring to boil and add shoyu, sugar, and ginger. Reduce heat to simmer. Add pork and gobo rolls; simmer 30 to 45 minutes, making sure liquid does not evaporate entirely. Add more water if necessary, but do not add more seasonings.

Trolling for Fish

The hot Okinawan climate made it difficult to preserve fish in the days before refrigeration, so despite being an island culture, Okinawans did not develop a devotion to seafood, unlike mainland Japan.

Fish was primarily eaten raw as sashimi. Any remaining pieces were either simmered in shoyu and sugar (nitsuke) or marinated in miso, sugar, and sake (misozuke) to extend its shelf life. Cooked nitsuke could be held two days at room temperature; misozuke for three to four days in a clay pot before cooking.

These days, given the benefit of refrigeration, fish dishes can be developed reflecting all the wealth of Okinawan flavors.

Fish Soup with Fermented White Soybean Paste

Yield: 8 portions

I grew up in a fishing family and we always had fresh fish to eat. I took pleasure in catching my share of near-shore reef fish, albeit small, with my bamboo pole. My grandma turned these fish into the best soup ever.

1 pound small reef fish (such as rock cod, mamo, kupipi, veke, papio), head on, scaled and gutted
2 tablespoons salt
12 cups water
3 pieces ginger, thinly sliced
¼ cup shiro miso (white miso)
½ cup green onions, thinly sliced

Cut fish in half or thirds and sprinkle with salt. Let sit 10 minutes. Rinse off salt and let fish dry a few minutes.

Place water in medium-sized pot and turn heat to high. Add fish and ginger; bring to boil, then reduce the heat to low and simmer 15 minutes, skimming impurities from surface. Add miso, stirring gently to dissolve miso without breaking fish pieces. Taste soup and add more salt if needed. Add chopped green onion and serve immediately.

Note: Fish may be removed from soup and served on the side if you prefer.

Grilled Fish with Sea Grape Salsa

Yield: 5 portions

Okinawans' legendary longevity is commonly attributed to diet, focusing on the consumption of bitter melon, sweet potato leaves, ginger, and seaweed. In fact, Okinawans consume more seaweed than any other ethnic group on the planet. This dish uses sea grapes (umi budoo), a type of seaweed that grows in Okinawa. The stems are covered with tiny spherical beads that have a crunchy texture and salty flavor. If you are unable to get fresh sea grapes, substitute salted semi-dried sea grapes that can be rehydrated in water. In Okinawa, fish is commonly eaten raw as sashimi or cooked nitsuke-style, so this grilled fish dish is very unique in texture and flavor. The best fish to grill would be firmer-fleshed fish such as m'ahim'ahi, ono, opah, 'ahi, or marlin.

Salsa:

1 cup umi budoo (sea grapes), coarsely chopped
1-ounce package shiofuki konbu (dried seasoned seaweed), julienned
½ cup tomato, small-diced
¼ cup onions, chopped
¼ cup okra, thinly sliced
1 tablespoon sesame oil
1 teaspoon shoyu (soy sauce)

5 (3-ounce) fish fillets
1 teaspoon salt
1 tablespoon vegetable oil

Combine salsa ingredients in a bowl; mix well. Set aside for 15 minutes.

Season fish fillets with salt; brush with vegetable oil. Grill to desired doneness. Serve fillets with salsa.

Kasutera Tamago Kamaboko
Fishcake with Egg

Yield: 5 portions

If the only fishcake you've ever tasted is store-bought kamaboko, you will be surprised by the depth of flavor and the delicate texture of a home-made loaf.

1 pound of boneless skinless white fish (mullet or bonefish)
1 tablespoon salt
8 whole eggs
6 egg yolks
1 tablespoon shoyu (soy sauce)
1 tablespoon sugar
½ cup mirin (sweet rice wine)
½ cup fish stock or dashi (Japanese broth)
2 tablespoons vegetable oil

Prepare a steamer or preheat oven to 350°F.

Grind fish in a suribachi (Japanese mortar and pestle) until almost smooth; add salt and grind again until smooth. Add eggs one at a time, making sure to grind each egg completely into the paste before adding the next. Add shoyu and sugar; mix until all the sugar is dissolved. Place mixture into a medium-sized bowl and add mirin and fish stock; mix until combined.

Use oil to grease a metal or glass loaf pan. Place fish mixture into pan. Steam 45 minutes or cover with foil and bake 45 minutes. Check for doneness by touching the center of the loaf gently; if the loaf springs back remove from heat and let rest 10 minutes. If a depression remains, cook longer.

To unmold, use a knife to loosen edges, then turn pan over to release the loaf. Slice into ½-inch pieces. Serve warm or cold.

Age Kamaboko
Fried Fish Cake

Yield: 8 portions

*T*he key is to this delicate pan-fried fishcake is to soak the grated carrots and gobo in water first to remove any excess color or bitterness, then squeeze it well to remove any excess liquid before adding it to the dish. The low and slow pan frying will create a light and fluffy "pillow" that can be eaten hot or cold.

- **1 pound of boneless, skinless, white fish (mullet or bonefish or snapper)**
- **2 teaspoons salt**
- **1 teaspoon sugar**
- **2 tablespoons mirin (sweet rice wine)**
- **4 eggs**
- **¼ cup carrots, grated and soaked in water**
- **¼ cup gobo (burdock root), grated and soaked in water**
- **3 tablespoons vegetable oil**

Grind fish, salt, and sugar into a smooth paste using a suribachi (Japanese mortar and pestle). Add mirin and grind another 30 seconds. Add eggs one at a time, making sure to grind in each egg completely before adding in the next.

Squeeze all liquid from grated carrot and gobo; fold into fish mixture.

Heat a small sauté pan on medium and add oil. Drop tablespoons of the fish mixture into the pan; flatten them a little to speed up the cooking process, if desired. Cook each "pillow" 5 to 7 minutes per side and serve hot or cold.

Katsuo No Tataki Gomae
Char Broiled Skipjack Tuna in Sesame Dressing

Yield: 5 portions

Charred rare tuna is cut and tossed in a sesame dressing in this dish that is similar in style to Hawaiian poke, but with an Okinawan flavor.

2 pounds aku (skipjack tuna) loin, boneless and skinless
1 teaspoon salt
1 tablespoon toasted goma (sesame seeds)
1 tablespoon sugar
1 tablespoon dashi (Japanese broth)
1 teaspoon rice wine vinegar
1 tablespoon shoyu (soy sauce)
1 tablespoon green onions, chopped
1 tablespoon katsuobushi (shaved dried bonito flakes)

Sprinkle aku with salt and quickly place under a broiler or on a grill. Char each side 30 seconds then remove to an ice bath for 1 minute to stop the cooking and keep center of the loin raw. Pat loins dry with paper towels, slice into ¼-inch pieces and place in a bowl.

Grind goma in a suribachi (Japanese mortar and pestle) to make a rough paste. Add sugar, dashi, vinegar, and shoyu; grind into a smooth paste.

Add paste to fish slices and mix to coat each piece well in sauce. Place in center of serving bowl and garnish with green onions and katsuoboshi.

Tuna Simmered in Soy Sauce

Yield: 5 portions

This dish utilizes the head and collar of the tuna, parts that are normally thrown away.

1 cup of awamori (Okinawan rice wine) or sake
2 cups dashi (Japanese broth)
3 cups leftover rafute braising liquid (or 1 cup soy sauce, 1 cup sugar, 1 cup plus 1 tablespoon grated ginger)
2 aku (skipjack tuna) heads or 1 yellowfin tuna ('ahi) head, cut into pieces 3 to 4 inches square, including the eyeballs (they are a delicacy)

Place awamori or sake, dashi, and rafute braising liquid in a wok or shallow pot. Add fish pieces and turn heat to medium. When liquid lightly bubbles, reduce heat to low and allow fish to simmer until meat separates from cartilage. Serve with liquid.

Sakana Misozuke
Miso-Marinated Fish

Yield: 5 portions

The miso-based marinade used in this dish is very popular in Hawai'i. Apply it to your favorite oily fish, such as butterfish, salmon, sea bass, skill fish, hamachi, kampachi, opah or cod. To add a twist, try this recipe with flavored miso instead of the regular white miso. Found in Asian or Japanese groceries, flavored miso most commonly comes with katsuo (bonito) and konbu (kelp).

½ **cup Okinawan brown sugar (see note)**
1 **cup shiro miso (white miso) or flavored miso**
½ **cup awamori (Okinawan rice wine) or sake**
1 **tablespoon grated ginger or 1 piece myoga (young ginger bud), thinly sliced**
5 **(3 ounces each) fish fillets**

Using a suribachi (Japanese mortar and pestle), grind/crush sugar into a smooth powder. Add miso, awamori or sake, and ginger; continue to grind until smooth.

Place fish fillets in a ziplock bag or glass dish and cover with miso mixture. Marinate one day for every inch of thickness of the fillets, up to three days.

When ready to cook the fish, remove fillets from marinade and place on a foil-lined pan. Broil 1 to 2 minutes per side, or until done.

Note: Okinawan brown sugar comes in cubes or blocks and needs to be crushed. If necessary, substitute granulated brown sugar in the same amount (no crushing necessary).

Noodles

Just Add Starch

Two main types of noodles are commonly eaten in Okinawa, soba and udon.

Soba is traditionally made from buckwheat flour in Japan, but in Okinawa wheat flour is used. Egg yolks are added to the dough to strengthen it, making Okinawan soba yellow in color compared to the brownish soba of mainland Japan.

continued on the next page

Udon is a thick wheat noodle commonly enjoyed in a hot or cold broth. Okinawans have used traditional Japanese udon as a substitute for the firmer soba in recent years.

Okinawan noodles were traditionally made in small batches that could be consumed in a short time to prevent spoilage. Today, soba and udon are made in larger batches, tossed in oil to keep them from sticking together and frozen for future use, as the process of making them can be time consuming.

The noodles can be enjoyed in broth with garnishes or stir-fried with protein and vegetables.

If you are purchasing commercially made noodles, it is a good idea to rinse them or drop them in boiling water for 30 seconds to remove any excess oil, especially if the noodles are going to be served in broth.

Okinawan Soba Noodles

Yield: 5 portions

*U*se these noodles in the Yakisoba recipe (page 82), or make the pork-based broth in the Soki Udon recipe (page 85) and use soba noodles in place of udon.

1 cup water
1 teaspoon baking soda
1 teaspoon salt
1 large egg plus 1 egg yolk
5⅓ cups bread flour
1 cup vegetable oil

Whisk together water, baking soda, salt, and egg in large bowl. Mix in flour, using your hands or a rubber spatula, in a folding motion. Once ingredients are combined but still crumbly, remove from bowl and knead on a smooth, flat surface for 20 minutes to develop the gluten in the dough to create a chewy noodle. Place dough in a plastic bag and allow to rest 2 hours.

Divide dough into 5 portions. Lightly dust work surface with flour and roll out each portion of dough into ⅛-inch thick sheets. Fold each sheet in half and cut the noodles to desired width. "Fluff" them by tossing them lightly by hand in a circular manner.

Fill a medium pot with water and bring to a boil. Cook noodles 2 to 3 minutes. Shock noodles in cold water; drain and toss in vegetable oil. Soba may be used immediately in soups or stir-fries, or portioned and frozen in ziplock bags or other containers for future use.

Udun Irichi
Fried Noodles

Yield: 5 portions

*U*don is a wonderful noodle that has a great texture and can be served in many ways. Leftover braising liquid from making rafute is used in this simple stir-fry, adding richness and giving the noodles a sticky gelatinous feel. But if you haven't been making rafute recently, an alternate sauce recipe is given.

1 tablespoons salad oil
4 ounces pork belly, thinly sliced
2 tablespoons garlic, chopped
1 pound udon noodles, freshly made or store bought
3 stalks green onion, cut into 1-inch pieces on a bias
½ cup rafute braising liquid (see note)

Heat a wok on high and add oil. Add pork belly and stir quickly to prevent scorching. Add garlic and noodles; stir-fry for a minute. Deglaze with rafute braising liquid and turn heat to low; stir in green onion and continue to cook for another minute. Serve immediately.

Note: Rafute braising liquid substitute: Combine 1 tablespoon shoyu (soy sauce), 2 tablespoons mirin (sweet rice wine), 1 tablespoon brown sugar and ¼ cup pork broth or dashi. Mix well to combine. Add all at once in place of rafute liquid.

Yakisoba
Fried Noodles

Yield: 4 portions

This is a local favorite. If you are unable to purchase prepared yakisoba sauce, make your own by mixing equal parts of red miso, sugar, soy sauce, and mirin (sweet Japanese rice wine).

2 ounces (1 cup) Spam, thinly sliced
1 teaspoon vegetable oil
8 ounces yakisoba noodles (fresh or purchased)
3 tablespoons purchased yakisoba sauce (preferably Bulldog brand)
1 cup cabbage, shredded
½ cup carrots, julienned
½ cup bean sprouts

Heat a non-stick pan on high; add Spam and little oil. Sauté until Spam is slightly crisp. Remove any excess oil, if desired, and add noodles. Stir until noodles are slightly crisp. Add yakisoba sauce, stir well, and reduce heat to low. Add cabbage, carrots, and bean sprouts; cook just until vegetables are slightly tender. Serve hot.

Soki Udon
Thick Noodles in Pork Broth with Mustard Cabbage and Braised Pork Ribs

Yield: 4 portions

*U*don was originally eaten in mainland Japan but has become a favorite of Okinawans as it can be eaten hot or cold, in broth or with dressing. If you cannot make your own udon, substitute store-bought noodles; or if they are unavailable in your area you may substitute ramen, saimin, or soba.

Udon noodles:
- 1 teaspoon salt
- 6 ounces (¾ cup) water
- 2½ cups all-purpose flour

Broth:
- 1 gallon water
- 1 piece dashi konbu (seasoned dried kelp)
- 2 cups katsuobushi (bonito flakes)
- ¼ cup sake (Japanese rice wine)
- 2 teaspoons salt

Braised ribs:
- 2 pounds pork ribs, cut into riblets
- ½ cup Japanese mirin (sweet rice wine)
- ½ cup sake (Japanese rice wine)
- 3 tablespoons shoyu (soy sauce)
- 1 carrot, cut into ¼-inch-thick slices
- 1 head mustard cabbage, cut into 1-inch squares

continued on the next page

To prepare noodles: Place flour and salt into a food processor; turn on and drizzle in the water slowly, just until mixture begins to combine. Knead dough for about 5 minutes, then allow the dough to rest 30 minutes. Roll into a sheet ¼-inch thick and cut into noodles ¼-inch wide and set aside.

To prepare broth and ribs: Place water, konbu, bonito flakes, sake, and salt into a large pot on low heat and simmer 30 minutes; strain liquid into a medium-sized pot and add pork ribs. Cover and simmer 30 minutes on low heat. Remove ribs and fat from liquid; set aside liquid. Place ribs and fat into a sauté pan with mirin, sake, and shoyu; simmer just until the liquid reduces by one-half. Turn off heat.

Meanwhile, place a medium-sized pot filled with water on high and bring to a boil. Drop in udon noodles and cook about 2 minutes. Strain, rinse slightly, and divide noodles into 2 large serving bowls.

Place carrots and mustard cabbage in reserved pork liquid and quickly bring to a boil. Season with additional salt, if needed. Arrange carrots and cabbage over noodles and pour 1 cup of broth over. Top with ribs as a garnish.

Buta Udun Irichi
Fried Thick Noodles with Pork

Yield: 5 portions

This wok-fried thick noodle dish can be supplemented with different vegetables—watercress, carrots, and shiitake mushrooms are great. If making this dish vegetarian, you may want to omit the ginger, as it is here to offset the strong odor of the pork, and replace it with garlic to help give the vegetables a savory aroma.

½ pound fatty pork belly, thinly
   sliced
1 tablespoon ginger, minced
2 (4- to 5-ounce) packages fresh or frozen udon noodles
1 cup green beans, cut into 2-inch lengths
1 cup karashina (mustard cabbage) leaves and stems, sliced
¼ cup dashi (Japanese broth) or water
1 tablespoon shoyu (soy sauce)
1 tablespoon oyster sauce

Heat a wok or pan on high. Add pork and cook 2 minutes to render fat. Add ginger and udon noodles; stir gently so noodles do not break. Add beans, cabbage, and enough water or dashi to moisten ingredients and prevent sticking. Add shoyu and oyster sauce; stir gently, just to coat the pork and noodles with the seasonings.

Vegetables & Salads

My mom is an incredibly wise woman who worked hard as a single mother to support us. I remember her telling me when I was six years old, "Grant, I may not be here to do things for you, so you have to learn how to survive on your own." She taught me to cook, wash the clothes, and clean the house.

I also remember walking to our community garden plot in front of the Honolulu Zoo on Kapahulu Avenue.

continued on the next page

There I would plant, weed, and pick vegetables. We grew many things, and harvested them, too. It was a different time and few people stole, as they do now.

My mom still tends her public garden plot near Ala Wai Elementary school, growing kabocha and hechima, vegetables I hated as a child, but love as an adult. Years ago the vegetables she grew were essential to supplementing a tiny income; today, although we could afford to buy our kabocha from a store, Mom's garden provides farm-to-table freshness.

Ta-Umu Ringaku
Sweetened Taro

Yield: 6 portions

Although this dish must cook for an hour, it is simple to prepare. The taro is boiled whole first, which makes it easier to slice and peel for the last stage of cooking.

1 pound taro
8 cups water
2 cups dashi (Japanese broth)
1 cup sugar
¼ cup awamori (Okinawan rice wine) or sake
2 tablespoons shoyu (soy sauce) or 1 tablespoon salt
Tangerine zest, for garnish

Place whole taro in water and boil 30 minutes. Let cool, then remove skin and slice into ¼-inch-thick slices.

Place dashi, sugar, sake, and shoyu in a sauté pan or wok; bring to boil, then reduce heat to low. Place sliced taro into pan and simmer 30 minutes, or until liquid reduces by three-quarters and taro is tender. Serve warm, garnished with tangerine zest.

Hechima no Chukafu
Simmered Loofa Gourd
Yield: 5 portions

Like kabocha, hechima requires gentle cooking to keep its delicate flesh tender, sweet, and intact. Over-cooking or cooking at too high a temperature will cause the flesh to disintegrate.

2 tablespoons vegetable oil

5 thin sliced ginger

8 (¼-inch-thick) slices kamaboko (cooked fishcake blocks) or chikuwa (tubes)

½ cup Tokyo negi (large green onion), sliced on diagonal

1 pound hechima (loofa gourd) cut into 1-inch cubes, skin and seeds removed

½ cup bamboo shoots, thinly sliced

2 cups dashi (Japanese broth)

1 tablespoon shoyu (soy sauce)

1 teaspoon sugar

1 teaspoon salt

¼ cup cornstarch

¼ cup water

2 eggs, lightly beaten

Heat a wok or sauté pan on high and add oil. When the oil lightly smokes, add ginger and quickly stir to prevent scorching.

Add kamaboko, Tokyo negi, hechima, and bamboo shoots; stir well. Deglaze with dashi (stir to loosen any bits stuck to bottom of pan); reduce heat to low. Add shoyu, sugar, and salt; simmer until hechima is just becoming soft and transparent.

Bring heat to high. Mix cornstarch and water to form a slurry. When liquid bubbles, add half the slurry to the pan and stir well to prevent lumps from forming. When liquid is thick enough to coat the back of a spoon, add egg and stir slowly to form "egg flowers." If the liquid is not thick enough, stir in remaining cornstarch slurry before adding eggs. Serve immediately.

Shirae
Crumbled Tofu Salad

Yield: 6 portions

This cold salad is often enjoyed as a vegetarian dish, but cooked proteins such as shredded crab meat or chopped cooked shrimp are good additions.

1 cup dashi (Japanese broth)
2 tablespoons mirin (sweet rice wine)
2 tablespoons shoyu (soy sauce)
1 tablespoon sugar
1 cup carrots, julienned
1 cup shiitake mushrooms, julienned
1 (10- to 12-ounce) block firm tofu
1 cup horenso (spinach) or watercress, blanched
2 tablespoons toasted goma (sesame seeds), plus more for
  garnish

Place dashi, mirin, shoyu, and sugar in a small sauté pan and bring to a boil. Add carrot and shiitake mushrooms; simmer 5 minutes, just until carrots are tender. Drain liquid and set aside to cool. Chill the carrots and mushrooms.

Cut or break the tofu block into small pieces. Place in cheesecloth and squeeze to remove as much water as possible. Place in a bowl and set aside.

Using a suribachi (Japanese mortar and pestle), grind goma about a minute, then add to cooled braising liquid and grind another minute. Pour over tofu and mix well, then add cooled cooked carrots, mushrooms, and blanched spinach. Toss lightly and garnish with toasted goma. May be served immediately or chilled and served.

Nankwa Ubushi
Simmered Kabocha Pumpkin

Yield: 6 portions

*T*his is a local island favorite. The key is to cut every piece of pumpkin to the same size and thickness to ensure even cooking. The braising liquid should never come to a boil, as this agitation may cause the pumpkin to disintegrate on the outer edges before it is cooked all the way through.

1 kabocha pumpkin (about 2 pounds), cut into 2-inch pieces, skin in on
2 tablespoons vegetable oil
¼ cup dried shrimp
4 cups dashi (Japanese broth) or water
2 tablespoons shoyu (soy sauce)
2 tablespoons sugar

Heat a wok or sauté pan on high and add oil. When the oil lightly smokes, add dried shrimp and stir quickly to prevent scorching. Deglaze with the dashi or water (stir to loosen any bits stuck to bottom of pan); add shoyu and sugar, stirring well until sugar is dissolved. Reduce heat to low and add pumpkin. Cover and simmer 30 minutes, or until pumpkin is tender.

Test for doneness by poking pumpkin with a toothpick; if the toothpick goes cleanly through, it is done. Serve warm or chilled.

Togan no Nishime
Simmered Winter Melon Stew

Yield: 6 portions

Togan, winter melon, is a favorite of Chinese and Filipino cooking as well as Okinawan and Japanese. Its mild flavor makes it a good canvas for many seasonings. In this preparation the classic Japanese flavors of dashi, konbu and soy sauce are augmented by brown sugar and chili peppers.

2 tablespoons vegetable oil
**2 pounds togan (winter melon), peeled, seeded, and cut into
   1½-inch cubes**
1 teaspoon ginger, minced
2 cups dashi (Japanese broth)
1 strip nishime konbu (thin kelp), cut into 1-inch lengths
1 tablespoon shoyu (soy sauce)
1 tablespoon brown sugar
2 chili peppers, split in half

Heat a wok or medium-sized pot on high; add vegetable oil. When oil lightly smokes, add winter melon and ginger; lightly sauté for 1 minute. Deglaze with dashi (stir to loosen any bits stuck to bottom of pan) and add konbu, shoyu, and sugar. Lightly stir, until sugar is dissolved. Add chili pepper, if desired. Simmer until winter melon is transparent and tender.

Papaya no Itaemono
Sautéed Papaya with Pork

Yield: 5 portions

This is a very simple but delicious dish. One note: If you use bacon or Spam instead of fresh pork, cut back on the amount of soy sauce, as both bacon and Spam contain a good amount of sodium.

½ pound pork belly or bacon, thinly sliced
1 pound green papaya, julienned
1 stalk scallions or Tokyo negi (large green onion), sliced on diagonal
1 (10- to 12-ounce) block firm tofu, drained well
2 tablespoons shoyu (soy sauce)
1 teaspoon mirin (sweet rice wine)
1 teaspoon chili pepper water, optional

Heat a wok or sauté pan on high; add pork belly or bacon. Stir well; cook 2 minutes to render fat. Remove pork or bacon from pan, save. Add papaya and scallions or green onions. Gently break tofu into bite-sized pieces using a spoon; add to pan.

Sauté until papaya becomes limp. Return pork or bacon to pan. Season with shoyu, mirin, and chili pepper water, if desired. Cook until most of the liquid is evaporated. Enjoy.

Tori Ni Shimun
Chicken Soup with Vegetables

Yield: 6 portions

*T*his very tasty chicken soup may be seasoned with salt or miso. Salt will enhance the chicken flavor while miso may mask that flavor, providing its own taste profile, so choose according to your personal liking.

2 pounds of your favorite chicken parts, bone in or boneless
1 tablespoon salt
8 cups dashi (Japanese broth) or water
1 tablespoon ginger, grated
1 cup zuiki (taro stems), sliced
1 cup hechima (loofa gourd), sliced
½ cup dry shiitake mushrooms, rehydrated in water and sliced
½ cup carrots, sliced ¼-inch-thick
1 cup karashina (mustard cabbage), cut into 1-inch pieces
Salt or miso, to taste

Place chicken in large bowl and sprinkle with salt; rub salt into chicken for about a minute.

Place dashi in large pot; bring to boil. Add chicken and let dashi return to boil, then reduce heat to low and skim off foam or scum floating on top of the liquid. Add ginger, zuiki, hechima, mushrooms, and carrots. Simmer 30 minutes, or until hechima is tender. Add mustard cabbage and season with salt or miso. Serve immediately.

Nasubi Unbuchi
Braised Eggplant

Yield: 5 portions

After making rafute (braised pork belly) you'll find yourself with a pot full of braising liquid. It's a shame to let all that flavor go to waste. Use it in this tasty eggplant dish.

3 long eggplants, cut diagonally into 2-inch lengths
1 teaspoon salt
½ cup cornstarch
⅔ cup vegetable oil
1 cup of Rafute braising liquid (Okinawan Braised Sliced Pork Belly, see page 53; or combine ¾ cup dashi, 2 tablespoons soy sauce, 2 tablespoons sugar, and 1 teaspoon grated ginger)
Pinch ground cayenne pepper
2 teaspoons green onions, chopped

Place eggplant in a bowl, sprinkle with salt, and toss to equally distribute salt. Add cornstarch and toss to evenly coat each piece. Place contents of bowl into a dry strainer and shake to remove excess cornstarch.

Place vegetable oil in a wok over medium heat. When oil lightly smokes, add eggplant and quickly pan-fry until pieces are lightly golden. Remove from pan and let drain on paper towels to remove excess oil.

Pour hot oil from wok into a metal container; return eggplant to wok over medium heat. Quickly add rafute braising liquid and cayenne pepper; allow eggplant to simmer until fully cooked (about 5 minutes). Remove to serving plate and garnish with chopped green onions.

Karashina
Pickled Mustard Cabbage

Yield: 4 portions

*P*ickled mustard cabbage can be eaten cold as a condiment, or added to a hot soup or stew to give it a kick! The pickled mustard cabbage can be held in the refrigerator for up to 3 weeks.

- 1 pound karashina (mustard cabbage), stems and leaves cut into bite-sized pieces
- 8 cups water
- 2 tablespoons salt
- 2 tablespoons vinegar
- 2 tablespoons sugar
- 1 chili pepper, crushed

Place the mustard cabbage into a plastic or ceramic container and press down firmly.

Place the water and remaining ingredients in a medium-sized pot and bring to a boil.

Pour the boiling mixture over the mustard cabbage and allow it to cool to room temperature, then store refrigerated.

When using the pickled cabbage, make sure to take out just what you need, squeeze out the excess marinade and serve as is or add it to your stir-fried pork dishes.

Desserts & Sweets

Andagi and More

When we think of dessert, we always think of sweets—it's a given. How we prepare the sweet items is another story. In Okinawa, where the wok has traditionally been a predominant cooking vessel, all Okinawan desserts are either fried or steamed.

Small, compact pieces of rice cakes, fried doughnuts or "popo" crêpes filled with brown sugar or candied coconut are always favorites, easy to hold and pop in the mouth.

Please feel free to create your own versions of these desserts with different flavorings, or serve them in a contemporary way, to take Okinawan desserts to the next level!

Grandma's Backyard Guava Jelly

Yield: Four 1-cup (½-pint) jars

I remember picking guavas and making jelly with Grandma during my "small-kid days." Grandma was the tall one back then, so my role was to pick ripe guavas from the lower branches, as well as those that Grandma dropped as she reached up high to pick from the top of the tree. I considered picking fruits in the backyard as playtime, but I now realize that it doubled as an unofficial cooking lesson. Forty years later, Grandma and I continue to pick guava and make jelly together, although our roles have changed. Now I reach for the fruit at the top of the tree and Grandma just picks what she can and waves "hi" to the neighbors.

10 cups ripe strawberry guava
3½ cups granulated sugar
½ pound paraffin wax

Wash guavas in cold water, remove stems, and crush guavas by hand or with potato masher. Place in a medium-sized pot; simmer 20 minutes. Turn heat to high and boil another 10 minutes, stirring constantly to prevent burning.

Set a large bowl beneath a colander lined with cheesecloth. Pour in cooked guava. Let guava strain "naturally" for 1 hour (pushing or forcing the pulp through the colander will make the jelly cloudy). You should have 2½ cups pure guava juice.

Place juice in a medium saucepan and add sugar. Quickly bring to boil, then slowly skim scum from the surface.

When bubbles become large, start testing the mixture by dipping a clean spoon into the center of the pan: If the mixture quickly sheets off the spoon it is not ready, but if it falls off in drops that "run together" then the jelly is ready.

Pour jelly into sterilized jars and top each with 2 ounces paraffin wax. The hot jelly will melt the wax so that it rises to the surface and covers the jelly completely. When the jelly cools and the wax hardens, cover the jars with their lids. Jelly may be stored at room temperature until jar is opened. After that it must be refrigerated.

     Sweets

Nantu
Old-Fashioned Glutinous Rice Cake

Yield: 8 portions

*I*n this Okinawan version of mochi, the mochiko-water mixture is first steamed, then incorporated with a sugar syrup.

2 cups mochiko (glutinous rice flour)
1¼ cups water
1 cup sugar
¼ cup water
½ cup katakuriko (potato starch) or kinako (ground roasted soy beans)

Place mochiko flour and water in a bowl; mix well until no lumps remain. Place mixture into a perforated pan or basket lined with a wet cheesecloth. Place pan or basket over a boiling pot of water or in a steamer; steam 45 minutes.

Meanwhile, combine remaining sugar and water in a small bowl; stir until sugar is dissolved. Mix hot steamed mixture with sugar mixture until combined; place in a container covered with a cloth until cooled, or let sit overnight.

Use a plastic knife to cut nantu into bite-sized pieces. Lightly toss in katakuriko or kinako to keep the pieces from sticking together.

Nantu
Contemporary Classic Rice-Flour Cakes

Yield: 8 portions

My version of nantu incorporates a rainbow of flavors and colors.

- 2 cups mochiko (glutinous rice flour)
- 1¼ cups water
- 1 cup sugar
- ¼ cup flavored liquid to match the extract used, or water
- 1 teaspoon flavored extract (coconut, watermelon, grape, etc.)
- 2 drops food color, matching the extract (yellow for pineapple or banana, red for watermelon, green for lime, purple for grape, etc.)
- ½ cup katakuriko (potato starch) or ground coconut

Combine mochiko and water; mix until smooth. Place into a microwave-safe bundt pan and microwave 5 minutes on high, or place in a covered steamer over boiling water and steam 40 minutes.

Combine the sugar with flavored liquid or water and stir well until all of the sugar is dissolved.

Combine cooked nantu with sugar syrup; mix well until combined. Place in a container and let cool before cutting. Dust cut nantu with katakuriko or ground coconut.

Benimo Nantu
Purple Sweet Potato Glutinous Rice-Flour Cake

Yield: 8 portions

This wonderful recipe can be enjoyed in many variations. Mashed kabocha, yams, or butternut squash can be substituted for the Okinawan sweet potato.

2 cups mochiko (glutinous rice flour)
1¼ cups water
1 cup benimo (Okinawan sweet potato), cooked and mashed
1 cup sugar
¼ cup coconut milk
½ cup ground katakuriko (potato starch) or kinako (roasted ground soy bean)

Combine mochiko and water in a bowl; mix well until combined. Place in a microwave-safe bundt pan and microwave 5 minutes on high or place in a covered steamer over boiling water for 40 minutes. Meanwhile, combine mashed sweet potato, sugar, and coconut milk; mix until smooth. Fold in cooked nantu until combined. Place in a pan, cover with a cloth, and let cool. Cut into bite-sized pieces and dust with katakuriko or kinako to keep pieces from sticking together.

Andagi, a Rare Treat

My childhood memories of andagi are few. My family only ate andagi at Okinawan Club picnics and at the Okinawan Festival.

Our family always participated in the festival with the Haebaru Club, representing Grandpa's hometown in Okinawa. We were assigned to work in many different booths, but I spent the last few years at in the andagi booth. I

Grandpa Akamine and I at the Okinawan festival Andagi Booth.

should clarify — it was the booth that sold the andagi. I have asked to work in the booth where the andagi is fried, figuring it would be a natural thing as I am a chef and very familiar with safety and sanitation. I was wrong. I was firmly told, "No men fry andagi." Call it sexist, call it discrimination, call it whatever you want, I never dropped or fried andagi at the festival.

Now I hold mini festivals in my own kitchen and I proudly drop and fry my own andagi. I've found that while oil temperature is critical, the batter is what will make or break you. My recipe calls for 1 cup of milk, and if you follow the recipe you will be satisfied. But if you like a sweeter andagi, use sweetened condensed milk, which also produces a more dense texture. Replacing the milk with sour cream creates a very fluffy, cake-like andagi.

Andagi batter has other uses. Lightly sweet, it pairs well with salty or sweet flavors. The andadog, the Okinawan version of a corn dog, and Waffle Dog, the famous hot dog in a waffle, are examples of creative uses of andagi batter.

Experiment, create, and enjoy!

Andagi or Sata Andagi
Okinawan Fried Doughnuts

Yield: 20 to 30 pieces, depending on size

This is a standard andagi recipe that results in a doughnut with a crispy outer shell and a cake-like center.

4 cups flour
½ teaspoon salt
1¾ cups granulated sugar
2 tablespoons baking powder
4 eggs
1 cup milk
1 teaspoon vanilla extract
Vegetable oil, for frying

Combine dry ingredients and wet ingredients (except oil) separately, making sure each is mixed well.

Add wet ingredients to dry and mix by hand until batter is smooth and thick. Chill 1 hour. (Batter can be chilled up to 3 days before frying.)

Add vegetable oil to pot to a depth of 4 inches; heat to 325°F. Carefully drop 2 to 3 tablespoons of batter by hand into the hot oil; fry until golden brown on all sides. Drain on paper towels to absorb excess oil.

Contemporary Okinawan Fried Doughnut

Yield: 20 to 30 pieces, depending on amount of batter used for each

This is a great way to create andagi of different flavors. The color of the added flavoring agent will alter the color of the finished andagi—fresh poi, for example, creates a dark brown andagi. If adding a dry flavoring such as matcha or cocoa powder, reduce the flour to accommodate the added powder (if adding 2 tablespoons of matcha powder, reduce the flour amount by 2 tablespoons).

4 cups flour
1 teaspoon salt
1¾ cups granulated sugar
2 tablespoons baking powder
4 eggs
½ cup mashed banana, sweet potato, kabocha pumpkin, etc.,
  or fresh poi
½ cup heavy cream
1 teaspoon vanilla extract
Vegetable oil, for frying

Combine dry ingredients and wet ingredients (except oil) separately, making sure each is mixed well.

Add wet ingredients to dry and mix by hand until batter is smooth and thick. Chill 1 hour. (Batter can be chilled up to 3 days before frying.)

Add vegetable oil to pot to a depth of 4 inches; heat to 325°F. Carefully drop 2 to 3 tablespoons of batter by hand into the hot oil; fry until golden brown on all sides. Drain on paper towels to absorb excess oil.

For the Love of Purple

My grandma is a lover of anything purple, so when it comes to home gardening, Okinawan sweet potato is a must.

The only problem is that the harvest is just once a year so you have to come up with creative ways to extend the shelf life of the potato to enjoy it over a period of time. Grandma experimented with freezing steamed sweet potato, which worked well, but only relatively so. The defrosted sweet potato was wonderful mashed, but somewhat soft and crumbly when simply sliced. So she decided to find ways to capitalize on her frozen stores of mashed potato.

Knowing that ohagi was a favorite of mine, but an expensive dessert to buy, she tried making it herself. Store bought an (bean paste) was expensive and too soft, making it difficult to mold. So Grandma decided to add mashed sweet potato to make the an easier to mold and to add her favorite color to the dessert. This version of ohagi became a hit and a family standard for holiday get-togethers.

Today, when she tells the story of her ohagi, Grandma insists that she created it out of necessity, using the mashed sweet potato to stretch the expensive an because her "mochi crazy" grandson would eat so many that the cost would bankrupt her.

On a family trip to Kaua'i when I was a 3 year old, I supposedly stole everyone's mochi, and devoured it as though I hadn't been fed for weeks. Grandma likes to remind me of that story. All these years later, I'll always have room for a sweet potato ohagi made with love!

Grandma and I at an Arashiro family reunion in Kaua'i, 1974.

Tumai Kuru Ohagi
Okinawan Sweet Potato Rice Cakes

Yield: 12 pieces

*O*hagi is a mochi-like dessert but made with whole rice grains rather than rice flour.

1½ cups mochi rice (glutinous rice)
½ cup medium grain white rice
3 cups water
1 tablespoon matcha (green tea powder)
3 tablespoons sugar
2 medium tumai kuru (Okinawan sweet potatoes)
1 (14-ounce) can tsubushi an (coarse-ground sweet red bean paste)

Combine both types of rice in a bowl and wash thoroughly. Make sure to drain all the water; let sit 3 hours. Place washed rice and the 3 cups of water in a rice cooker and cook.

Steam sweet potato 40 minutes.

Combine cooked rice with matcha and sugar; stir well. Let rice to cool to room temperature, then form into 12 egg-shaped "bullets."

Mash cooked sweet potato and mix in tsubushi an. Place a 12-inch-square piece of plastic wrap on a plate and place ½ cup of sweet potato mixture in center. Spread sweet potato mixture into an oval about ¼ inch thick and place a rice bullet in the center. Carefully lift edges of the plastic wrap and mold the sweet potato mixture evenly around the rice to form the ohagi. Repeat to make 12 ohagi.

Note: Instead of using a rice cooker, you could steam the rice at the same time as the sweet potatoes. Be sure to put the rice in a separate layer above the potatoes to ensure that the rice will not be discolored by purple potato liquid.

Okinawan Sweet Potato Fritters

Yield: 10 portions

These fritters are a family favorite. Their crispy, crunchy shell hides a soft, sweet purple center that melts in your mouth! Enjoy it alone or with vanilla ice cream.

1 cup tumai kuru (Okinawan sweet potato), cooked and mashed
¾ cup mochiko (glutinous rice flour)
½ cup sugar
½ teaspoon salt
½ cup water
Vegetable oil, for deep-frying

Combine all ingredients, except oil, in a bowl; mix well. Place in a gallon-sized ziplock bag, flatten bag to a thickness of ½ inch and place in freezer until frozen solid (about 5 hours).

Heat oil to 325°F. Remove frozen potato mixture from ziplock bag in a solid sheet. Cut into ½-inch by 3-inch fritters. Immediately deep-fry until golden brown. Place in a paper towel-lined container to absorb excess oil. Enjoy!

Shikuasa Sorbet
Okinawan Lemon Sorbet

Yield: 5 portions

This is a great frozen treat that is refreshingly sweet and sour. Use an ice cream machine to form a smooth sorbet, or freeze the mixture in a pan and scrape it with a fork to make a shikuasa granita. If you cannot find shikuasa in your local Japanese market, you may substitute calamansi or tangerine.

1 cup shikuasa (Okinawan lemon) juice, (about 6 fruit)
½ cup water
1 cup sugar
¼ cup corn syrup
1 tablespoon shikuasa zest
1 teaspoon salt

Wash and zest shikuasa, then squeeze out the juice. Combine ingredients in a bowl and stir to dissolve sugar. Place mixture in ice cream machine and churn just until the consistency of the mixture resembles soft mashed potatoes.

Remove mixture from machine and place in a plastic container. Freeze solid overnight.

Shikuasa Curd Tarte

Yield: 1 tarte, 12 portions

10 ounces of your favorite sugar dough
4 ounces white chocolate, melted
5 ounces sugar
3 whole eggs + 2 yolks
4 ounces unsalted butter
Pinch salt
½ cup shikuasa (Okinawan lemon) juice
1 cup whipped cream
12 raspberries
12 mint sprigs

Roll out the sugar dough into a circle ¼-inch thick and place it in the tarte mold. Prick the bottom of the shell to prevent it from rising or bubbling during baking. Bake at 325°F for 12 minutes or until golden brown.

Place chocolate in a double boiler and melt completely.

Remove shell from oven and immediately brush entire shell with white chocolate. Let cool to room temperature.

Place sugar and eggs in a bowl and whisk well to combine.

Melt butter on low heat in a medium pot and add salt and shikuasa juice. Add some of the hot mixture into the bowl containing the sugar and eggs and mix well to temper, then add the contents of the bowl to the pot and stir well making sure it does not burn on the bottom.

Once the mixture reaches 180°F, the eggs will coagulate and thicken the mixture. Once this happens, pour into cooled tarte shell. Refrigerate 4 to 6 hours to set the curd.

Place whipped cream in a pastry bag with a star tip and pipe out 12 rosettes. Top each rosette with a raspberry and mint sprig.

Okinawan Lemon Curd and Okinawan Sweet Potato Parfait

Yield: 8 portions

A fun treat that can be made in any type of glass or plastic container, this dessert is perfect for a family buffet. The shikuasa curd can be put into a pie shell and chilled for four hours or overnight to form a shikuasa curd tarte.

½ cup shikuasa (Okinawan lemon) juice
½ cup sugar
3 whole eggs plus 2 yolks
4 ounces unsalted butter
Pinch salt
1 cup tumai kuru (Okinawan sweet potato), cooked and mashed
2 tablespoons sugar
¼ cup coconut milk
1 cup whipped cream

Place shikuasa juice, sugar, and eggs in small saucepot and mix until sugar dissolves. Turn heat to low and slowly stir with a whisk to prevent curdling. As mixture heats it will begin to thicken; add butter and continue to whisk vigorously until all of the butter is melted into the curd. Add salt; stir 30 more seconds, then remove curd from the pot and place in a ceramic or plastic container. Chill.

Place sweet potato, sugar, and coconut milk in a small bowl and whisk until smooth and shiny.

Using 8 shot glasses, place 1 tablespoon whipped cream in each glass. Layer with 2 tablespoons sweet potato mixture, then 1 more tablespoon whipped cream. Top with 2 tablespoons shikuasa curd. Served chilled.

Goyacha Crème Brûlée
Bitter Melon Tea Crème Brûlée

Yield: 6 portions

*T*his very interesting dish utilizes dehydrated goyacha, a goya tea that makes this dessert very mild and soothing—and not at all bitter. The heavy cream is added after the tea bags steep to prevent it from scorching and curdling.

2 cups milk
3 bitter melon tea bags
2 eggs
14 egg yolks
3 ounces sugar (about ⅓ cup)
3 cups heavy cream
1 tablespoon vanilla extract
¼ cup sugar, for topping

Place milk in a small pot and bring to boil; turn off heat and add tea bags. Let steep 15 minutes.

Pre-heat oven to 300°F.

Place eggs, yolks, and sugar in a bowl and whisk until sugar dissolves.

Remove tea bags and add cream and vanilla extract; turn heat to medium. When milk and cream mixture starts to gently bubble, add ⅓ of the mixture to the egg mixture and stir vigorously to combine. Add egg mixture to pot with heated milk and cream; continue to cook on medium heat while stirring constantly until slightly thickened.

Divide evenly among 6 ramekins or bowls about 3 inches in diameter. Place ramekins or bowls into a 2-inch deep pan filled halfway with water. Place the pan into the oven for 45 minutes.

Let ramekins cool to room temperature or chill overnight. To serve: Top each with a little extra sugar and torch or place under a broiler to caramelize sugar, forming a caramel top or "brûlée."

Contemporary Creations

My modern dishes incorporate different tradition-al Okinawan recipes to form new, exciting, and complex dishes that can be enjoyed as a part of a high-end meal, as individual small plates, as appetizers passed at a holiday party, or on a buffet table at a family potluck. As I grow and evolve I like to revisit past ideas and take them to a new, higher level.

Enjoy these modern creations. I hope they inspire you to create your own unique dishes with Uchinanchu flair!

Mini Okinawan Soft Tacos

Yield: 8 portions

created this as a small appetizer using ingredients not widely consumed due to their unique characteristics. I hope that more people will enjoy them in this form. The goya namashi and mimiga in this recipe should be squeezed well, to remove excess liquid that will cause the crêpe to deteriorate and tear.

- **8 chive or scallion stalks, blanched**
- **8 cooked Hirayachi (Chive Crêpes, see page 5), 3 inches in diameter**
- **1 cup Goya Namashi (Pickled Bitter Melon Salad, see page 34), squeezed well**
- **1 cup Mimiga (Marinated Pigs Ear, see page 45), squeezed well**
- **2 tablespoons tobiko (red flying fish roe)**

Lay 1 blanched chive stalk horizontally in front of you. Top with 1 crêpe, centering crêpe over chive stalk. Place 2 tablespoons pickled bitter melon salad in center of crêpe and flatten it. Top with marinated pigs ear, then tobiko.

Gently grab each end of the chive stalk and pull upward. Tie chive stalk into a knot and trim the excess stalk with scissors. Repeat to make 8 tacos.

Makizushi Uchinanchu
Rolled Okinawan Sushi

Yield: 3 rolls

No matter how carefully you cook, you're bound to end up with some imperfect bits and pieces of a dish. My version of rolled sushi uses overcooked, slightly shredded, or disintegrated pieces of sliced pork and pumpkin left over from other dishes. Think of this as a contemporary Okinawan version of the seasoned rice enjoyed as kimbap in Korea and makizushi in Japan.

3 sheets nori

3 cups Sushi Gohan (Okinawan Vinegared Rice for Sushi, see page 17)

1 cup Shirishiri (Fine Julienne Vegetables Stir Fry with Egg, see page 21)

1 cup karashina (mustard cabbage) in Gomae (Ground Sesame Seed Dressing, see page 3)

½ cup Andansu (Rendered Pork Miso Paste, see page 48)

1 cup Nankwa Ubushi (Simmered Kabocha Pumpkin, see page 94), mashed into a paste

1 cup Rafute (Okinawan Braised Sliced Pork Belly, see page 53), shredded

Place a sushi rolling mat on a cutting board. Place nori on the mat with the shiny side down. Place 1 cup sushi rice in center of nori sheet; gently spread rice into a uniformly thin layer on the bottom two-thirds of the sheet.

About an inch from the bottom of the rice-covered nori sheet, place thin rows of ⅓ cup carrot, ⅓ cup pumpkin, ⅓ cup mustard cabbage, 2 heaping tablespoons pork miso, and ⅓ cup shredded pork, making sure each row is of uniform thickness and extends from the left to the right edge of the sheet.

Gently lift the bamboo mat from the bottom, being careful not to disturb the nori, rice or toppings. Roll away from you, until you reach the area of the nori that is bare. Sprinkle a little water on this part of the nori, then continue to roll until you reach the end of the sheet. Remove sushi roll from mat and place with the seam down for 5 minutes. Continue to make 2 more rolls. Slice each roll into 8 pieces.

Chive Crêpe topped with Spinach in Sesame Dressing and Sliced Braised Pork

Yield: 8 portions

Somehow the ability to pick up a tidbit and enjoy it in a couple bites seems to make it tastier. This dish was created to turn leftovers from the previous night's dinner into something new and exciting. Sliced braised pork (rafute) is a favorite that can never be made in a small batch, so it is a good source of leftovers to work with in this way.

8 cooked Hirayachi (Chive Crêpes, see page 5), 5 inches in diameter
1 cup horenso (spinach) in Gomae (Ground Sesame Seed Dressing, see page 3)
16 slices Rafute (Okinawan Braised Sliced Pork Belly, see page 53)

Place 1 cooked crêpe in center of small plate. Mound 2 tablespoons spinach in sesame dressing in center of crêpe. Top with 2 pieces rafute, slightly overlapping them.

Inari Uchinanchu
Trio of Stuffed Cone Sushi

Yield: 9 individual cone sushi

Cone sushi (inarizushi) is another favorite of mine. The sweet flavor of the marinated fried tofu skin is addicting, and when you fill each shell only halfway with rice you can fill the remaining space with your favorite stuffing. I've seen this done with spicy 'ahi and ocean salad mix, but for a true Okinawan, these fillings will surely please.

9 prepared inari cones
2 cups Sushi Gohan (Okinawan Vinegared Rice for Sushi, see page 17)
1 cup Goya Namashi (Pickled Bitter Melon Salad with Octopus, see page 34)
1 cup Shirishiri (Fine Julienne Vegetables Stir Fry with Egg, see page 21)
1 cup Shirae (Crumbled Tofu and Crab, see page 93)

Divide rice evenly among cones and press into bottom halves of cones. Stuff 3 cones with bitter melon salad, three with zucchini/bell pepper sauté, and 3 with tofu and crab. Serve 1 of each type of stuffed cone on a plate as a trio.

Okinawan lacquerware, or shikki, is known for its distinctive red color and designs that incorporate island motifs such as the hibiscus, coral, and palm trees. It's made using wood from deigo trees indigenous to Okinawa. Pig's blood is used as a primer, which results in a highly durable coating.

Goya Chawan Mushi to Mozuku Ankake
Bitter Melon Egg Custard with Gelatinous Seaweed Sauce

Yield: 5 portions

My version of Japanese-style chawan mushi (steamed egg custard) incorporates bitter melon tea, a less-familiar product available in local Asian markets.

2 bitter melon tea bags
3 cups hot water
½ teaspoon salt
4 eggs
½ cup mozuku (thin Okinawan seaweed)
1 teaspoon shoyu (soy sauce)
1 tablespoon constarch dissolved in 1 tablespoon water to
　　make a slurry
5 bitter melon chips
5 chive flower stalks

Steep tea bags in hot water 15 minutes. Remove tea bags and stir in salt until dissolved. Pour 1 cup of tea into a small sauce pot; set aside.

Crack eggs into a medium-sized bowl. Stir in remaining 2 cups tea until combined. Divide mixture among 5 glass or ceramic cups. Steam about 8 minutes in a covered steamer over boiling water.

Meanwhile, bring the reserved cup of tea to boil. Add mozuku and shoyu; drizzle in the cornstarch slurry, stirring well to prevent lumps from forming.

Remove cups from steamer. To serve: Top each cup with a thin layer of the thickened seaweed sauce and garnish with a bitter melon chip and chive flower.

Okinawan Eggs Benedict

Yield: 2 portions

*E*ggs Benedict is a favorite breakfast dish of mine, so I decided to make my own version with an Okinawan flair. The dish has the same basic components as the classic—starch layer, pork layer, egg layer, and butter-based sauce on top. I hope you enjoy it as much as I do.

> 1 tablespoon vegetable oil
> ½ cup Andagi batter (Okinawan Fried Doughnut, see page 110)
> 4 pieces Rafute (Okinawan Braised Sliced Pork Belly, see page 53)
> 2 eggs
> ½ cup Rafute braising liquid (Okinawan Braised Sliced Pork Belly, see page 53)
> ½ cup cold butter
> 2 thinly sliced pieces myoga (ginger bud)

Heat a small non-stick pan on high and add oil. When oil lightly smokes, pour andagi batter to form 2 small discs in pan. Reduce heat to low; allow batter to cook and rise until a golden brown ring appears on the bottom edge of each pancake. Flip pancakes and continue to cook until golden brown on the other side.

Place each pancake in center of a small plate and top each with 2 pieces of rafute.

Cook eggs as you like them. I enjoy sunny-side up, but over-easy, over-medium, over-hard, scrambled, or poached are fine. Place 1 cooked egg on top of the rafute slices on each plate.

Place rafute braising liquid in a small saucepan and quickly bring to a boil. Turn off the heat and quickly whisk in cold butter to create an emulsion. Top each egg with 3 to 4 tablespoons of this sauce and garnish with thinly sliced ginger bud (myoga).

Karashina Natto Sarada
Pickled Mustard Cabbage and Fermented Soy Beans

Yield: 10 portions

*T**his dish is commonly eaten on small nori sheets or chive crêpes.*

½ cup Karashina (Pickled Mustard
    Cabbage, see page 101)
½ cup natto (fermented soy beans)
½ cup yamaimo (crushed mountain yam)
¼ cup raw okra, sliced
½ cup 'ahi (tuna), small diced
2 shiso leaves, cut into thin strips
½ cup Rafute liquid (Okinawan Braised Sliced Pork Belly,
    see page 54)
1 tablespoon shikuasa juice (Okinawan lemon)

Place the mustard cabbage, natto, yamaimo, okra, and 'ahi in small mounds next to each other in center of a shallow bowl or dish. Sprinkle with shiso.

Combine rafute liquid and shikuasa juice in small bowl; mix well. Spoon this sauce around the dish or plate. Serve with small sheets of nori or Hirayachi (Chive Crêpes, see page 5).

Stuffed Goya Braised in Miso

Yield: 5 portions

This dish reflects the Chinese influence on Okinawan cuisine—from the use of the wok to the ground pork filling commonly found in steamed or fried dim sum.

Filling:

- 1 cup ground pork
- 1 egg
- ½ cup shiitake mushroom, minced
- 1 tablespoon garlic, minced
- 1 tablespoon ginger, minced
- 1 tablespoon shoyu (soy sauce)
- 2 tablespoons cornstarch

- 2 pieces goya (bitter melon) cut into 4 pieces, each with seeds removed to form an empty cylinder
- 4 cups dashi (Japanese broth)
- 2 tablespoons shiro miso (white soy bean paste)
- 2 tablespoons mirin (sweet rice wine)
- 2 tablespoons cornstarch slurry to thicken (equal parts cornstarch and water)

For filling: Combine ground pork, egg, shiitake mushroom, garlic, ginger, shoyu, and cornstarch in a bowl and mix well. Stuff goya cylinders with equal amounts of the filling mixture.

Heat dashi in a medium pot; add miso and mirin; stir until dissolved. Bring to a boil and add stuffed goya; reduce heat to a simmer. Cook 15 minutes, then remove goya to a platter.

Thicken remaining braising liquid with cornstarch slurry, then pour thickened sauce over the stuffed goya to serve.

Okinawan Waffle

Yield: 2 portions

The versatility of the basic Okinawan fried doughnut batter (andagi) is showcased here. When cooked in a waffle iron, the batter forms a crispy outer shell with a soft cake-like interior. Eat them alone or with your favorite topping.

1 cup Andagi batter (Okinawan Fried Doughnut, see page 110)
½ cup Grandma's Backyard Guava Jelly (see page 104)
½ cup softened butter
2 tablespoons sugar
1 tablespoon liliko'i (passion fruit) purée
½ cup whipped cream
½ cup fruits, chopped

Heat a waffle iron and spray each side with nonstick spray. Pour andagi batter into center of iron and close.

While waffle is cooking, place butter in small bowl, add sugar, and whisk until light and fluffy. Whisk in liliko'i purée. Set aside.

Remove waffle from waffle iron; cut in half and place each half in center of a plate. Top each waffle half with jelly, butter, whipped cream, and fruits.

Glossary

*Note: **Purple** terms are Uchināguchi (Okinawan language)*

Aburage: Deep-fried soft tofu commonly sold in rectangular or triangular shapes with a light and airy internal structure

'Ahi (maguro): A generic name for tuna in Hawai'i—'ahi could refer to yellowfin tuna, big-eye tuna, or bluefin tuna

Aku (katsuo): Hawaiian name for bonito or skipkack tuna

Andansu or **anda insu:** Okinawan pork bean curd paste made from pork, sugar, miso, and ginger

Andagi or **sata andagi:** Deep-fried Okinawan doughnut that is spherical in shape, featuring a crispy crust and a dense, cake-like inner structure

Araimo: Dasheen or mini Asian taro, which becomes very slippery and slimy once it is peeled and comes into contact with water

Ashitibichi (tonsoku): Pig trotters, including the foot and lower shank

Awamori: Okinawan distilled whiskey or wine made from grain, potato, or rice

Azuki: Asian red bean commonly sold dried

Benimo or **beni imo (satsuma imo):** A general term for sweet potato; can refer to the golden or purple varieties

Bojishi: Okinawan name for the loins and center back cuts of the pig

Champuru: Stir-fried dish, usually containing vegetables and tofu

Chibijiri: Okinawan name for the ham or hindquarters of the pig

Chin pin: Sweet rolled crêpes also known as "popo" crêpes

Chiraga: Okinawan name for the head of the pig

Chiribira (nira): Common chives that are solid green with white flowers, not to be confused with garlic chives that have a purple tinge and lavender flowers

Dashi: Japnese broth or soup stock made from water, katsuoboshi, and konbu

Dekuni (daikon): Long white radish

Fuchiba (yomogi): Mugwort

Fuisaga: Okinawan name for the upper shank of the pig

Gobo: Burdock root

Gohan: Cooked rice

Goma: Sesame seeds that can be white or black

Goya (nigauri): Bitter melon

Haraga: Okinawan name for the center belly or bacon of the pig

Hechima: Loofah gourd, a fibrous natural plant is pared and commonly used as shower "scrubs." The young plants are edible (aka nabera)

Hihatsu: Okinawan chili pepper, similar in size and heat to a jalapeño

Horenso: Spinach grown and sold as whole heads; cooked with leaves and stems attached

Hyotan: Long squash with off-white flesh and large internal seeds

Imu or **nmu:** Potato

Insu (miso): Fermented soy bean paste that comes in white (shiro miso) or red

Insunaba (fudanso): Swiss chard or rainbow chard

Irichi: A term to describe items stir-fried in a wok

Jubako: A lacquerware box used for food presentation that can come in one, two or three layers

Jushi: Rice gruel that can also have many added ingredients

Kabocha or **nankwa:** Common name for the common green Asian pumpkin; sometimes referred to as nankwa, the Okinawan name for all pumpkins

Kamaboko: Block form of cooked fish-cake commonly with a bright pink outer layer and white interior

Kanduba or **kandaba:** Okinawan sweet potato leaves

Kampyo: Dried strips taken from the flesh of round edible gourds

Karashina: Mustard cabbage

Katakuriko: Potato starch used to coat or dust glutinous rice cakes (mochi or nantu) or confectionaries

Kinako: Toasted soybean powder used to coat or dust glutinous rice cakes (mochi or nantu)

Kiri kubu (kiri konbu): Thinly sliced dried kelp

Kubu (konbu): Large, thick kelp commonly sold dried

Kubujiri: Okinawan name for the shoulder of the pig

Konnyaku: Japanese cooked gelatinous cake made from the starch of a lily tuber

Koshi an: A puréed, smooth, sweetened red bean paste

Matcha: Finely ground green tea powder that can be made into tea but is also used as a flavoring agent for syrups, sauces, pastries, and ice cream bases

Mimiga: Okinawan name for the pig's ear or pig's ear dishes

Mirin: Sweet rice wine used for cooking

Miso: Fermented soy bean paste that comes in two varieties white (shiro miso) and red (aka miso) red miso, the red being slightly saltier with a metallic iron flavor

Mitsuba: Trefoil, leafy green plant aka "Japanese parsley." It is often used as garnish for Japanese dishes.

Mochi: A cake made from pounded, steamed glutinous rice, or a cake that is steamed or baked, made from glutinous rice flour. Both forms can be made with or without fillings.

Mochiko: Glutinous rice flour used to make glutinous rice cakes (mochi or nantu)

Muchi (mochi): Glutinous rice cake with or without filling

Myoga: Young ginger bud

Nabera (hechima): Loofa gourd or loofa squash

Namashi (namasu): A salad containing ingredients marinated in rice wine vinegar, sugar and salt

Nankwa (kabocha): Okinawan term for pumpkin

Nanohana: Rapeseed plant blossoms, slightly bitter greens

Nantu: Steamed, baked, or microwaved sweetened glutinous rice cake

Nashibi (nasubi): Okinawan name for eggplant, usually refering to the long purple variety, but other varieties as well

Nigari: Magnesium chloride, derived from ocean water, is available for purchase in Japanese markets or on-line sites such as eBay or Amazon.

Nimum: A cooked dish of any kind

Nishimi (nishime): A simmered dish that may contain beef, pork, or chicken and a variety of vegetables in a broth seasoned with soy sauce and sugar

Nishimi kubu (nishime konbu): Thin kelp strips usually used to wrap items (kubu maki), tied in knots and simmered (nishime) or to make a braising liquid (nishime)

Nori: Dried sheets of pulped seaweed called laver

Ogo: General name for crunchy varieties of thin seaweed found in near-shore waters

Panko: Japanese style of bread flakes or crumbs that can be coarse or finely ground

Popo: White crêpes usually filled with brown sugar or andansu

Rafute: A pork dish simmered in broth, soy sauce, sugar, and ginger

Ramen: Japanese name for curly, thin, wheat-based noodles commonly served in a hot broth seasoned with salt, soy sauce, or miso

Sake: Japanese rice wine

Saimin: Japanese name for a thin, straight, wheat-based noodle commonly served in hot broth or wok-fried

Sashimi: Sliced raw fish or other seafood, or other thinly sliced items served raw

Sengiri daikon: Thin, dehydrated strips of daikon that must be rehydrated before cooking

Shiitake: Sawtooth oak mushroom, available fresh or dried. The dried varieties are preferred as they have a savory "smoky" flavor when rehydrated.

Shibui (togan): Large winter melon, commonly served as a soup vessel in China

Shikuasa: Citrus fruit with qualities similar to orange, lemon, or kalamansi

Shimun (shiru): Soup or broth of a simmered dish

Shingiku: Leafy green of an herb in the chrysanthemum family

Shoyu: Soy sauce, a condiment brewed from fermented roasted soy beans and wheat

Soba: Thick noodle made from buckwheat flour. The Okinawan version uses eggs; the Japanese does not.

Sokibuni: Okinawan name for pork spareribs

Somin (somen): Fine wheat- and rice-based noodles

Tako: Japanese name for octopus

Takuan: Pickled daikon, commonly colored yellow

Taumu: Taro corm commonly grown in the Pacific region

Tempura: Battered deep-fried vegetables or proteins

Tobiko: Flying fish roe

Togan: Winter melon

Tofu: Soy bean cake made from heated soy milk curdled with magnesium chloride (nigari).

Tsuyu: Soy sauce-based concentrated flavoring agent used to make a dipping sauce for tempura, somen, or soba

Tsubushian: Roughly mashed sweetened red bean paste; may contain whole or larger pieces of red beans

Tui (tori): Chicken

Tumai kuru (benimo or beni imo): Okinawan purple sweet potato

Uchinagani: Okinawan name for the flap or lower filet of the pig

Udun (udon): Thick wheat-flour noodles that can be eaten cold with tsuyu or hot in a broth

Ukara (okara): Cooked, ground soy beans; a byproduct of the tofu making process

Umukuji: Sweet potato starch

Unbushi: Another term for a one-pot dish

Usachi (sarada): Salads

Wakame: Young, tender seaweed

Warabi: Fiddlehead ferns

Wasabi: Japanese horseradish grown in calm river waters

Yachidofu (yakidofu): Fried tofu cubes (not to be confused with aburage)

Yakisoba: Wok-fried thick soba noodles

Yasei (yasai): General term for vegetables

Yuba: Dried or dehydrated skin that forms on the surface of heated raw soy milk; another by product of the tofu-making process

Zuiki: Mountain taro stems

Vegetables

About the Author

Grant Kiyoshi Sato's passion for cooking and especially Okinawan food came early in his life growing up with his grandmother in Kaimuki. As a youngster his artistic interests were drawing and painting, and, as a teen, sculpting. But then his culinary side took over. Graduating from Kapi'olani Community College's (KCC) Culinary Arts Program he began teaching culinary arts in 1998. (He was the 2000 Francis Davis Award winner for Excellence in Undergraduate Teaching in the University of Hawai'i System.) In 2003, he started the Grant Sato Scholarship fund. Currently, he is a Chef Instructor at KCC in addition to being the Host and Co-Executive Producer of the popular cooking show *What's Cooking Hawai'i*. Taking Hawai'i cooking to the next level and making it an art form to express oneself are his current passions. Grant regards his career and life as a work in progress.

Other titles in the series

6 x 9 in. • Hardcover, wire-o binding

A Korean Kitchen explores a popular cuisine that relies on many vegetables, grains, fermented foods, and simple cooking techniques that require little fat. Meats are served as a small part of this vegetable-centric cuisine that focuses on many tasty side dishes on the table. Food writer Joan Namkoong draws on her island heritage to explain the Korean kitchen in Hawai'i, distinctly different from a Korean kitchen in Korea. (180 pp.)

A Portuguese Kitchen shares traditional recipes done Hawai'i-style by Wanda A. Adams. Portuguese cooking is at its heart very, very simple. The cuisine relies on the freshest, most carefully selected ingredients. It is comforting, but not edgy, earthy, sumptuous, and tasty. Find recipes for traditional Bacalhau (salt cod), Portuguese soup, Linguica Pica (spicy Portuguese sausage), Arroz Verde (Green Rice), Milho Frito (Fried Cornmeal Porridge), and more. (192 pp.)

A Japanese Kitchen by Muriel Miura explores the essence of Japanese cooking, from Zensai (appetizers) to Okashi (desserts). There are many centuries-old recipes updated and Westernized to meet today's tastes and lifestyles, and others that more clearly reflect the 150-year legacy of the Japanese in Hawai'i. It includes detailed background information, cultural insights, family vignettes, and essays on Japanese traditions and celebrations. Food historian Arnold Hiura's introduction shows how Japanese cooking has evolved in Hawai'i. (272 pp.)

A Chinese Kitchen provides insights into Chinese food traditions, culture, and experience in Hawai'i. Lynette Lo Tom captures the delicious cooking of her mother, extended family, and friends. There is a wide range of dishes including Winter Melon Soup, Chinatown-style Crispy Skin Roast Pork, and Mongolian Beef. Most of the recipes are Cantonese, as three-quarters of the Chinese workers who came to Hawai'i to work on the plantations were from Zhongshan (a part of Canton Province, now called Guangdong). (216 pp.)

A Filipino Kitchen shows the diverse richness of colors, tastes, and flavors that define Filipino cooking and reflects Chef Adam Tabura's favorite childhood meals. Many of Adam's island-style recipes show new twists on traditional dishes. Plantation-style dishes are given a Filipino touch and Filipino dishes are given a tropical flavor. These recipes will appeal to those familiar with Filipino food and serve as a great introduction for those who want to learn more. (184 pp.)

To order these titles and more, visit
www.mutualpublishing.com

Notes